UNCHARTED HORIZONS
A JOURNEY OF RESILIENCE

An Autobiography by
Dr. Sarath Jayawardana

© Copyright 2025 - All rights reserved.

The contents of this book may not be reproduced, duplicated, or transmitted without the direct written permission of the author or publisher.

Under no circumstances will the publisher or author be held liable for any damages, recovery, or financial loss due to the information contained in this book neither directly nor indirectly.

ISBN: 978-1-7638779-1-7

TABLE OF CONTENTS

FOREWORD 4

PREFACE 9

Chapter 1: The Seeds of Determination 13

Chapter 2: Rebellion, Revelry, and Revelations 38

Chapter 3: Medical School and Medical Career in Sri Lanka 50

Chapter 4: The Janatha Vimukthi Peramuna Insurrection of 1989 and Leaving My Motherland 92

Chapter 5: Opportunities and Legal Tribulations in Australia 120

Chapter 6: Striving for Excellence in My Professional and Personal Lives 143

Chapter 7: Navigating Health Concerns 185

Chapter 8: What Made Me Who I Am? 200

PRACTICAL INSIGHTS FOR READERS 211

ACKNOWLEDGMENTS 216

ABOUT THE AUTHOR 217

FOREWORD

Uncharted Horizons: A Journey of Resilience is an autobiography detailing the adventurous and exciting life journey of Dr. Sarath Jayawardana in Sri Lanka and Australia. It describes Sarath's life experiences, including a harrowing account of the insurrection and civil war that traumatised Sri Lanka in 1989 and his emigration (or escape) to Australia in 1990. Although his Memoir documents the horrors of that country's insurrection, it is nevertheless an uplifting story that celebrates the values of hard work, persistence, dedication, faith, and determination to succeed in unfamiliar, even hostile, environments.

Although I do not harbour a principled objection to the writing, reading, and assessing of autobiographies–in fact, I enjoy reading autobiographies because they provide fascinating insights into the lives of their authors–I am often suspicious about their contents and wary of the interpretations of reported events. Although autobiographies offer interesting, and sometimes surprising, insights into the achievements and failures of their authors, they may contain biased recollections of their achievements.

Autobiographies are usually important, not for what they contain but for what they omit. They typically do not disclose embarrassing information and may well fail to elaborate on unpleasant aspects of their authors' lives because revelations are embarrassing or implicate other people who may still be alive and be aggrieved at the inclusion of their involvement.

But this autobiography is an honest narrative. It objectively discusses the achievements and failures of its author, who is an accomplished professional having obtained degrees and qualifications in medicine and in law in Sri Lanka, Australia, and St. Kitts in the West Indies.

Life experience discloses that there are two kinds of people: builders and destroyers. A builder is a person who builds upon the foundations laid by their predecessors and uses these foundations to build new programs that benefit society. By contrast, a destroyer disrespects traditions and values developed by their ancestors. Even a perfunctory reading of this autobiography reveals that Sarath is a builder who, during his professional life, sought to constantly establish new organisations and programs that serve the interests of society. He provided the comforts his family deserves, whilst assuaging his professional curiosity and nurturing his ambition.

This "building" mentality is evidenced by Sarath's establishment and stewardship of the Australian Institute of Holistic Medicine (AIHM), later rebranded as the Australian Institute of Higher and Further Education (AIHFE), and his unstinting efforts at developing the establishment into a reputable, educational institution for the study of complementary medicine. Sarath opines that "The excitement of creating something transformative outweighed the fears."

Sarath also describes his service as the President of the Sri Lankan Cultural Society in Western Australia as one of the highlights of his life. His narrative of the many events organised during his presidency inevitably will cause readers to consider the benefits of Australia's multicultural policies. In this context, a prominent Australian commentator, Professor Lauchlan Chipman had earlier fanned suspicions about the "multicultural" agenda. In his influential essay, *The Menace of Multi-Culturalism*, Chipman made a distinction between "soft" multiculturalism–the food, dances, and cultural festivals of an ethnic group–and "hard" multiculturalism, which prescriptively seeks to impose rules of behaviour on people. He argued that "hard" multiculturalism:

> ... is about the preservation of 'ethnic integrity', the reinforcement and imposition on the new-born of sets of traditions, beliefs, and values which include, as well as those which are noble and enlightened, some which are at least as inhuman, as grotesquely ignorant, and as racist, as sexist, and as bigoted as any that can be squeezed from even the most appalling of ockers.[1]

However, this autobiography proves that Sarath always maintained an open and welcoming attitude to any person, regardless of race, ethnicity, or religious affiliation. Hence, there is no doubt that his association with the Sri Lankan Cultural Society represents the best of multiculturalism. Indeed, his enthusiastic narrative shows that multiculturalism can play a significant role in the maintenance of socially cohesive and tolerant Australian values. But I suspect that, regardless of what people think of multiculturalism, Sarath is vitally aware of the need for Sri Lankans to integrate into the wider Australian society.

Sarath describes his joy at becoming a Knight of Malta: it was one of the success stories of his distinguished career, alongside his medical school graduation in Chicago in 2011 and the conferral of a law degree by the University of New England in 2018. However, there were also serious challenges, notably his legal battles with the medical establishment that sought to stifle his acupuncture practice in Western Australia. He characterises the dispute as a test case to ascertain whether, and if so to what extent, the practice of acupuncture is a medical procedure. His

---

[1] Lauchlan Chipman, 'The Menace of Multi-Culturalism, *Quadrant*, vol. 24, No. 10, October 1980, 3 at 5.

account of the litigation is riveting and reveals the extent to which the law may occasionally be commandeered to achieve a partisan outcome.

His autobiography also vividly recalls the challenges posed by the development of the Institute of Holistic Medicine and his unsuccessful attempt at achieving accreditation by TEQSA for his proposed bachelor's degree in naturopathy.

Sarath's detailed treatment of his unexpected and brutal battle with a serious cardiac ailment is a ubiquitous reminder of the brittleness of life.

One remarkable insight offered by this enthralling story is the importance of a happy marriage in the development of a successful career. Throughout his book, Sarath is effusive about the supporting role played by his wife. Specifically, he states that one of the many remarkable qualities of his wife "is her belief in my ideas, no matter how ambitious or unconventional they might be. She has been a steadfast partner in my journey, helping when she could, advising when necessary, and trusting me to chart our course."

Insightful reflections and advice are offered throughout the autobiography. These reflections are an opportunity for the author to ruminate about the happenings in his life and learn from them.

It is a book about faith, freedom, entrepreneurship, hard work, achievement, and imagination: these are precisely the kind of values Australia needs to maintain its prosperity and attraction to new migrants.

This autobiography will be valued by people who are interested in world affairs, medical advances, law, education, multiculturalism, and faith, and who still believe in the power of goodness, decency, Australian fair play, and/or are looking for inspiration.

Sarath's book documents his search for excellence, expressing it very eloquently as follows:

> Learning, surrounding myself with excellence, expressing gratitude, and maintaining a growth-oriented mindset have been the principles that shaped my decisions and defined my life. They are not just values I hold; they are the essence of who I am. These beliefs have taught me that life is not about perfection but progress, and for that, I remain eternally grateful.

I am confident that Sarath's autobiography will become a classical study of a remarkable and successful migrant journey. It will certainly be read eagerly by people who are seeking to emulate a role model business leader when developing their businesses. Especially Sri Lankans who live in Australia and around the world, as well as all those who have an interest in international events, will welcome the opportunity to read and learn from this fine autobiography.

Gabriël A. Moens AM

Emeritus Professor of Law

The University of Queensland

January 1, 2025

PREFACE

Life is a journey of transformation, a path where challenges test our resilience and intentions to shape our destiny. I have walked this path of transformation from a small village in Sri Lanka to building a life of fulfilment and purpose in Australia. This story is my gift to you–an account of how boundaries can be broken, dreams can be achieved, and adversity can be transformed into opportunity.

As a young boy growing up with limited resources, I was entrusted with an extraordinary gift: freedom. My parents gave me the freedom to choose, dream, and lead. This freedom became my compass, guiding me through a life marked by challenges and prospects. From forming a community organisation in my village to attending a prestigious medical school, I learned early on that determination and intention are our most powerful tools.

When political turmoil forced me to leave my homeland in 1990, I arrived in Australia with little more than a vision for a better future. It was a leap into the unknown: yet it set the stage for building a life driven by education, community, and the pursuit of excellence. Since founding an education and wellness institute that trained hundreds of students to pursue careers in health and wellness, my journey has been a testament to the power of perseverance and the courage to dream.

This book is for those standing at a crossroads, uncertain of their next steps going forward. It is for the newly arrived migrant seeking to find their place in an unfamiliar world, for the professional striving to overcome barriers, and for anyone seeking inspiration to turn limitations into stepping-stones. Through my life story, I want to show that we can shape our destiny with firm determination and commitment, no matter where we come from.

As you read these pages, I invite you to reflect on the possibilities in your own life. Let my experiences serve as a reminder that adversity, when met with courage and intention, can be a catalyst for growth and transformation.

I owe my journey to those who stood by me, believed in me, and challenged me. To my parents, who gave me the freedom to choose my path and trusted me to find my way. To my siblings, who cared for me when I needed it most. To my teachers, mentors, friends, patients, students, and clients, who have been my guides and sources of inspiration. To my wife Luckmalie, who has been my companion and trusted friend through every twist and turn, and to my beautiful children Poornima, Chaturanga and Kalpana, who have challenged me to see life from new perspectives.

A special acknowledgment goes to my daughter, Kalpana, for her relentless encouragement to write my story and for her thoughtful feedback.

To Dr. Ajith Mendis, the late Professor Anton Jayasuriya, and Dr. Andrew Ong, whose guidance and support came at the most critical turning points of my life.

My heartfelt gratitude also extends to my dear friend and respected academic Professor Gabriël Moens AM for generously dedicating his time to editing my manuscript, providing a thoughtful Foreword for this book, and encouraging me to write.

I am deeply grateful to my editor, Blair Parke, for her invaluable assistance in the final editing and proofreading of this book, ensuring it is free of errors.

This autobiography is not just my story—it is a legacy, a testament to the belief that no matter the obstacles, we can create lives of purpose, fulfilment, and joy. I hope this book inspires you to embrace your journey, break through your own barriers, and find the strength to achieve your dreams.

Welcome to my story. May it inspire yours.

Sarath Jayawardana

January 1, 2025

Where I was born, grew up, educated and worked

Untitled layer

Kahawatta

Kotakethana

Pelmadulla

Faculty of Medicine, University of Colombo

Colombo South Teaching Hospital (Kalubowila)

Teaching Hospital - Badulla

Divisional Hospital (B) - Badalkumbura

Keppetipola

Nuwara Eliya

Panadura

I have highlighted where I was born, brought up, educated, lived and worked

CHAPTER 1
The Seeds of Determination

I was born on October 21, 1956, in the tranquil village of Polwatta, near Weligama, in the southern province of Sri Lanka. My mother gave birth to me in her family home where she was born, a place that embodied the serene charm of rural life. The back of the house opened directly onto the banks of the Polwatta River, its gentle waters flowing like a lifeline through the village. This river, with its rhythmic currents and soothing sounds, was more than a geographical feature–it was a source of nourishment, inspiration, and connection for the community.

Polwatta was a village of rare beauty: its pristine white sand, scattered abundantly across the landscape, sparkled in the sunlight. At the same time, tall coconut trees swayed gently in the tropical breeze, their green fronds casting dappled shadows on the ground below. Just a short distance away, the breathtaking Weligama beach stretched along the coastline, with its golden sands merging into the turquoise waters of the Indian Ocean. The village was also steeped in spirituality, surrounded by numerous Buddhist temples whose tranquil presence added an air of peace and reflection to daily life.

I was the second of six children in our family born to my parents, a lively household that experienced both joy and loss. My siblings included two sisters and two brothers; a third brother, born just a year after me, passed away at birth. His passing, though not a memory I hold, cast a quiet shadow over our family, a subtle reminder of life's unpredictability and the strength needed to survive adversity.

My maternal grandfather was a man of influence and respect in Polwatta. Though I was too young to fully grasp the extent of his stature, I recall the deference with which villagers sought his advice. His wisdom and leadership shaped the lives of many around him, leaving a legacy that resonated within our family.

Shortly after my birth, our family relocated to Kotakethana, a small village nestled amidst the lush hills of the Ratnapura District. Kotakethana was surrounded by sprawling tea plantations, their terraced slopes forming a lush green blanket over the hills. In the valley below, vibrant paddy fields thrived, their bright green hues shifting with the seasons. These fields, interwoven with the rhythms of rural life, shimmered like mirrors during planting season and later swayed with ripening stalks in the breeze.

At the boundary between the village and the tea plantation stood my father's grocery shop, a vital community hub. Unlike the typical corner store, his shop was a bustling centre of activity, offering groceries, clothing, garments, and even a tea and coffee corner. It was where villagers and tea plantation workers came together, making the shop a social and economic focal point.

My earliest memories are intertwined with the shop's aromas of spices, textiles, and fresh food, forming a mosaic of sensory wonder. I vividly remember the vibrant colours of the goods, the rhythmic flow of customers, and the hum of conversations that filled the air. The shop's environment, though modest, felt alive with the stories and struggles of the people who passed through its doors.

My sister and I initially lived in a single room tucked within the shop itself. The close quarters, while challenging, sparked boundless imagination and curiosity for us. The shop was more than a place of business; it was both our home and the stage where my childhood dreams began to unfold.

As my father's business flourished, he built a three-bedroom home close to the shop, offering our family more space to grow. Yet even with this improvement, I often yearned for something beyond the immediate confines of Kotakethana. While the shop was a testament to my father's success, its physical boundaries nurtured my growing desire to explore a world beyond the village, the tea plantations, and the paddy fields. I dreamed of broader horizons where my aspirations could take root and grow.

These early days, framed by the serene beauty of Polwatta and the industrious spirit of Kotakethana, laid the foundations for my character. My family's nurturing environment, my birthplace's unique charm, and my childhood's industrious setting all fuelled a quiet determination within me to rise beyond the life I knew and explore the boundless possibilities that lay ahead.

The foundations of learning and imagination

My early education began in the village school, a humble yet formative setting where my curiosity about the world began growing. I studied there up to grade three before transferring to Kahawatta Primary School, about 2.5 km away from my home; it was a step that broadened my horizons and introduced me to a more structured learning environment. My village school was a simple affair, with basic facilities and teachers who were as much mentors as disciplinarians. Despite its modesty, it was a place where seeds of learning were sown, and my imagination was nurtured.

One incident from my village school remains etched in my memory forever. The principal, a stern but kind man, once asked me what I thought was the favourite, or main food, of a butterfly. Without hesitation, and with the innocent confidence of a young child, I answered, "Cake." I honestly believed I had provided the correct answer, associating the butterfly's delicate beauty with something as sweet and joyful as cake. The principal did not correct me; instead, he shared the story with my father later, and, together, they laughed heartily. Only then did I learn the truth: A butterfly's primary food is flower nectar. This moment, though humorous, was a gentle introduction to the importance of curiosity, humility, and the lifelong process of learning.

My father was a man of immense discipline and unwavering dedication. Every day, he rose at 4:30 a.m. to begin his work at the shop. Around 5 a.m., he would spray the shop with turmeric water, a practice rooted in tradition and believed to cleanse the space of negativity. The fragrance of Sambrani smoke soon followed, as its curling wisps filled the air, purifying the shop and creating a calm, almost sacred atmosphere.

The early mornings were a ritual for him, not just a habit but a testament to his work ethic, which prepared the shop for business and infused it with a sense of sanctity and purpose. My father would then light an oil lamp before a small Buddha statue and chant prayers with quiet reverence. This ritual, which took about 15 to 20 minutes, was more than a routine: it was an act of devotion, a way of beginning and ending his long, demanding days with gratitude and mindfulness. The same rituals were repeated each evening around 8 p.m., when the shop closed. These moments, though seemingly simple, reflected his belief in the role of spirituality and practical endeavour–a philosophy that guided much of his life.

My father had a warm personality, treating everyone with kindness and respect, and earning the admiration of neighbours and customers alike. My father's life was a testament to discipline, hard work, and unwavering commitment.

Beyond his hard work, my father also had a gift for storytelling. His tales, rich with imagination and a touch of mystery, captivated all who listened. One story that stands out is his account of a rabbit he encountered on a dark road one night when he was cycling. He claimed it was not an ordinary rabbit but a ghostly apparition that darted in front of his bicycle, vanishing into the shadows as he passed. As a child, the story fascinated and frightened me in equal measure. It left a deep impression on me, blurring the lines between reality and the supernatural.

This tale resurfaced in my mind one day when I was riding a bicycle with a friend on a dark evening. We were enjoying the freedom and adventure that came with exploring the village roads when suddenly, my bicycle tyre punctured. As we stood stranded on the side of the road, the memory of the ghostly rabbit flooded my mind.

Fear overtook reason, and I abandoned the bicycle, running home as fast as I could. Halfway there, the realisation hit me: Returning home without the bicycle would mean facing my father's displeasure, a consequence far worse than any phantom hare. Summoning my courage, I turned back, chanting loudly to ward off imagined spirits, and pushed the bicycle all the way home once I found it again.

In terms of my foundation for learning, as children, my siblings and I were expected to help at the shop whenever we were not in school. This usually meant assisting with tasks early in the morning before school and returning to lend a hand after classes. While I dutifully showed up in the mornings, I often found excuses to avoid the shop in the evenings. The repetitive nature of these responsibilities sometimes felt burdensome to me, and when I was asked to participate in the opening and closing rituals, my reluctance grew stronger. I did not fully appreciate the significance of these rituals at the time, viewing them more as tedious tasks than acts of devotion. Yet, looking back, I see how these tasks were deeply woven into my father's sense of purpose and the rhythms of our family life.

Though I helped my father in the shop from an early age, assisting with opening and closing, serving customers, and handling the counter, I knew deep down that running my own store was not the life I wanted. The shop, while essential to our family's livelihood, felt like a boundary–its walls confining my dreams. The routines, though valuable in teaching me discipline and responsibility, could not contain my yearning for something more.

The push bicycle, however, offered me a glimpse of freedom, becoming more than a means of transportation; it was a vehicle that provided opportunities and offered possibilities for escape. Riding through the village, feeling the wind on my face, I caught glimpses of a world much larger than Kotakethana. The tea plantations, the paddy fields, and the winding roads whispered promises of exploration and growth.

These early experiences shaped my sense of self and my aspirations. While my father's discipline and storytelling instilled values of hard work and imagination, my own encounters with fear, freedom, and the vastness of the world beyond my village sparked a desire to explore and grow. It was in these small yet profound moments that the seeds of my dreams were planted, a longing to push past boundaries and embrace the unknown.

My father worked tirelessly, often clocking twelve-hour days in the shop. However, despite the hard labour, he maintained a steady demeanour, earning him the respect and admiration of the village. His shop was more than a business; it was a cornerstone of the community, a place where locals gathered not just to buy necessities but to exchange stories, share news, and seek advice.

One aspect of our household that left a lasting impression on me was the pervasive influence of the caste system, a traditional social hierarchy primarily rooted in India, dividing people into groups based on hereditary roles, occupations, and social status. My mother, though loving and devoted, held firm beliefs about caste distinctions. She would label certain individuals as belonging to "lower" castes and avoided, or was reluctant to engage with, them. While my father did not openly practice these distinctions, my mother's attitudes were evident in her interactions.

I was deeply unsettled by this practice and often found myself challenging her on the matter. Even as a young boy, I felt a strong sense of justice and fairness. Everyone deserved equal respect, regardless of their social standing. My arguments with my mother about caste distinctions, though perhaps simplistic at the time, were early expressions of a rebellious streak that would later fuel my drive to challenge societal norms and pursue broader ideals as part of my life and career.

A man of strength and principles

My father was a man of quiet strength and principles, the only licensed gun holder in the village–a status that brought him a certain level of prestige. Yet, despite owning a gun, he never used it for hunting or inciting violence. The only times I saw him wield it were during his occasional shooting practices, aiming at trees to maintain his skills. For him, the gun was less a weapon and more a symbol of safety and dignity.

This sense of security may have been influenced by a tragedy in his past. I heard that his younger brother was killed in a knife attack by another villager when I was very young. While I have no memory of the incident, I imagine it left a profound impact on my father, shaping his cautious and disciplined approach to life moving forward.

My father was a man of moderation, as he did not consume alcohol and adhered to the Buddhist precepts, maintaining a moral compass that guided his actions. While he was not a temple-going Buddhist, his daily practices and rituals reflected a quiet, personal faith. His actions spoke louder than any sermons because he lived by example, treating others with respect and leading a life of integrity.

He employed several local boys in the shop, giving them both a livelihood and a sense of purpose. This not only earned him the loyalty of those who worked for him but also the respect of the entire village. His employees and customers alike admired his fairness and warmth. All our male siblings were addressed as Mahattaya (Sir), my sisters as Nona (Madum), and our mother was similarly respected and addressed as Hamine (Madam).

These small gestures of respect reflected the high regard in which our family was held in our village. Yet, my father's respectability was not born of wealth or influence alone: it was his character, his work ethic, and his kindness that elevated him in the eyes of the community.

These early experiences, observing my father's rituals, values, and interactions with others, left an indelible mark on me. They taught me the importance of discipline, respect, and acting on one's principles. Even as I resisted certain aspects of the life he built, I carried forward the lessons he imparted, lessons that would shape my own journey and aspirations in profound ways.

Family bonds and formative experiences

Family played a vital role in shaping my early years, not just through my immediate household but also through the extended network of relatives who came and went. Each of them brought with them a unique influence, leaving an impression on my young mind.

One of the most significant presences in my early childhood was my mother's youngest brother, my uncle, Chandrasena. We called him "Baby Mama" (he was the baby uncle, as he was the youngest boy in his family). He came to stay with us when I was about two years old. In his twenties at the time, he had a kind and energetic presence that made him an instant favourite of mine. I later learned that it was my father who helped secure him a job in a nearby tea estate plantation, a field job that offered both stability and opportunity. For years, my uncle was a cherished part of our household, blending seamlessly into the family dynamic.

I especially looked forward to visiting him at the plantation with my mother during school vacations. By then, he had moved to another tea estate near Ratnapura, having earned a promotion and started a family of his own. Despite his new responsibilities, my uncle never failed to treat me with warmth and generosity, often slipping a few rupee notes into my hand before we left. It was a gesture that, though small, filled me with immense delight. His kindness and affection made him my favourite uncle, a status he holds to this day.

Our home was often a haven for relatives seeking opportunities or support, like my uncle, and my mother's cousin was another important figure during this time. She came to live with us while taking up a teaching position at a school near our home. Once again, it was my father who played a role in helping her secure the teaching job. Her presence in our home brought a new dynamic to our household, as she became not only a role model but also a close confidant to me. Her gentle demeanour and nurturing spirit made her my favourite aunt.

She stayed with us for several years, during which she became an integral part of our family. Her dedication to her students and her quiet resolve to pursue a career inspired me, even if I did not fully realise it at the time. Her example planted seeds of appreciation for education and perseverance in me, values that would later guide my own ambitions toward a future career.

My mother's sister also came to live with us and stayed until our parents arranged her marriage. She was a delight, bringing joy to our household. She not only assisted my mother with household duties but also lovingly took care of the five of us. My parents took charge of her wedding arrangements, ensuring everything was meticulously planned for her new chapter in life. After her marriage, she left our home, but the cherished memories of her presence added warmth and depth to the tapestry of relationships that shaped my childhood.

The bicycle: A symbol of freedom

One of the most liberating moments of my youth came when I learned to ride my father's bicycle. I was about 11 or 12 years old, and the bicycle–an old, sturdy model with a luggage rack–was both a practical tool and a symbol of freedom. On the day I managed to ride a short distance without placing my feet on the ground, I felt an overwhelming sense of achievement. It was as if I had unlocked a new level of independence to my life.

The bicycle became more than just a mode of transport; it was a gateway to freedom. Later, for a brief time, I even rode my bicycle to attend high school in Pelmadulla, a journey of about ten kilometres one way. Though the route was long and the ride occasionally exhausting, it gave me a taste of the world beyond my immediate surroundings.

However, my father's bicycle, with its utilitarian design, felt inadequate for the image I wanted to project to others as a teenager. Borrowing a friend's modern bicycle, sleek and stylish, I rode to school with a newfound confidence. Those rides, though brief in the grand scheme of things, felt like an adventure–moments of escape and self-discovery that fuelled my growing dreams of a future unbounded by the constraints of my village life.

These experiences–sharing our home with relatives, observing their aspirations, and embracing my own small triumphs–taught me the value of connection, generosity, and determination.

Each moment, whether tied to family bonds or personal milestones, added depth to my understanding of the world. They showed me that life, while rooted in tradition and responsibility, held endless opportunities for growth and exploration. These lessons, drawn from the everyday fabric of my childhood, became the foundation upon which I began to dream of horizons far beyond the familiar roads of Kotakethana.

A childhood filled with people and purpose

Reflecting on my childhood, I am struck by the generosity and hospitality of my parents, especially my father. Our home was rarely empty, often filled with relatives, community members, and those seeking temporary refuge or opportunity. My father had an innate sense of duty toward family, extending help not just to my mother's relatives but to his own as well. I can recall one of my father's cousins living with us for an extended period, seamlessly becoming part of our family's daily life.

This spirit of generosity extended beyond the members of our family. Our home became a haven for those in need, including the local government agent representative, the Gramasevaka, who was offered a room in our house. His modest office operated from that room, blending official duties with the warmth of a household setting. Later, our home also provided shelter to the local midwife and several schoolteachers from the northern regions who worked in the nearby state plantation schools. These teachers, far from their own families, found a sense of belonging within our walls, enriching our home with their presence and stories.

For me, this bustling household was a source of joy, as I relished the company of the many people who came through our doors, each bringing their unique stories and perspectives. The constant hum of activity made our home feel vibrant and alive, teaching me the value of community, kindness, and shared responsibility.

Unfortunately, our village, though charming in its simplicity, was marked by its lack of infrastructure. There was no electricity, and transportation posed significant challenges to people getting around. To reach the nearest town, we either walked 2.5 kilometres or crossed a river using a makeshift tree bridge to catch the local bus. While these obstacles were a part of daily life, they became a source of deep frustration for me as I grew older.

As a teenager, I could not accept that these hardships were unchangeable in my village. Determined to make a difference, I formed an organisation called Navodaya (meaning "New Dawn"), rallying the villagers to address these issues collectively. Our initial focus was building a proper road to connect the village to the outside world. Fundraising efforts, community meetings, and hands-on work followed, though not without resistance. Some local farmers strongly resisted our roadwork, fearing the removal of the fences they had erected across the road to protect their paddy fields from cattle would lead to the destruction of their fields. They were unwilling to consider alternative solutions to safeguard their harvests and repeatedly rebuilt the fences cut into the road, obstructing our progress. Nonetheless, we remained determined and pressed on in building the roads.

Even after I left the village, my brothers continued the work we had started. Today, the road we envisioned is a reality–an accessible path that stands as a testament to the determination and unity of our community. Alongside the road came electricity, transforming the village and easing the lives of those who live there. These achievements remain a source of pride, a tangible reminder of the power of collective action.

The impact of family

Amid the challenges of village life, some of my most cherished memories are of visits to my maternal grandparents' home in Polwatta. Nestled along the Polwatta River, their house was a place of boundless joy and comfort. Behind their house, the river flowed serenely, its banks lined with an abundance of Kirala trees bearing delicious fruits. My siblings and I would roam the riverbank, picking and eating Kirala fruits to our hearts content.

Our stays in Polwatta were filled with laughter and the warmth of family. My grandparents, aunts, and uncles welcomed us with open arms, creating an atmosphere of love and indulgence. Meals were a particular highlight, featuring local delicacies like fish curry cooked with grated fresh coconut, accompanied by rice and a variety of other flavourful curries. Dessert often included natural yoghurt paired with treacle and a refreshing drink made from wood apple, which we enjoyed in abundance.

My father ensured that our visits to Polwatta were pleasant. He would hire a car, and we would travel in relative comfort, a rare luxury for us. At that time, it was just the four of us—my mother, father, sister, and I—as my other siblings had not yet been born. Together, we would embark on these trips, and for a few days, life felt carefree and magical. Although my father's hometown of Midigama was near Polwatta, I do not recall visiting it. Polwatta, with its tranquil river and welcoming family, became my sanctuary of happiness.

These experiences–living in a bustling household, navigating the limitations of village life, and finding joy in family visits–shaped my perspective on resilience, community, and the pursuit of betterment.

Whether through the lessons of hospitality demonstrated by my parents or the sense of fulfilment from building something lasting for my village, these moments enriched my understanding of life's purpose. They taught me that even in the simplest settings, there is potential for greatness. The bonds we form, the challenges we overcome, and the joys we embrace all contribute to the stories we carry forward.

Despite the vibrant atmosphere at home, my parents kept a close watch on my movements and interactions, especially until I reached the age of 12 or 13. Their cautious nature meant that I was largely limited to friendships formed at school, leaving me with little connection to other children in the village. While this restriction sometimes felt stifling, it also strengthened my bonds with my siblings and cultivated my imagination.

My childhood was not without its playful moments. I fondly remember the simple yet thrilling games I shared with my younger brothers. One of our favoured games involved pushing a discarded tyre with two sticks and racing it down the dirt paths of the village, while competing to see who could maintain the best control of the tyre. I enjoyed playing hide-and-seek with my sister, who was two years my senior, or pretending to be a doctor and nurse. We built make-believe houses while my sister "cooked" imaginary meals that we would pretend to savour. These innocent moments of creativity and camaraderie remain some of my most treasured memories.

During my school years, I enjoyed a level of independence that was unusual for children of my age. My parents, despite their cautious approach to my interactions within the village, trusted me to make decisions about my education, friendships, and the path I wanted to follow. This freedom was a gift, allowing me to explore my interests and develop a sense of responsibility early in life. For that, I am deeply grateful to them.

At Kahawatta Primary School, my talents for leadership, public speaking, music and singing quickly began to surface, and my teachers played a pivotal role in recognising and nurturing them. They encouraged me to participate in speech competitions, drama, music, and sports, creating opportunities for me to shine. I gained confidence as I took on leadership roles, becoming a familiar and respected figure within the school community.

One of the highlights of my primary school years was being nominated by teachers for roles in the student council, where I was elected as president and held the position for several years. This leadership experience was transformative, teaching me how to organise, motivate, and work collaboratively with others.

My teachers went above and beyond during this time, dedicating extra time to prepare me for speech and debating competitions. Their patience and guidance paid off, as I frequently returned victorious from events, carrying with me not only medals but also an increasing belief in my own abilities. Beyond the podium, I was active in sports teams, art projects, and the school music group, all of which helped me hone a wide range of skills. These experiences instilled in me a love for public speaking, creativity, and teamwork–qualities that would prove invaluable to me in the years to come.

I still consider my time at Kahawatta Primary School one of the most significant periods of my life. It was there that the foundation of my character was laid, shaped by the encouragement of mentors who believed in me. Their influence remains a beacon of gratitude in my heart, for they saw potential in me even before I fully understood it myself.

Thankfully, not all my school memories were tied to achievements. Like many children, I experienced the innocent, and sometimes perplexing, emotions of early attraction to the opposite sex. I was intrigued by the mystery and charm of my female classmates, occasionally finding myself drawn to one or another. Yet, these feelings were fleeting, and if the interest was reciprocated, my emotions would shift as quickly as they had emerged.

These early crushes, while inconsequential in the grand scheme of life, were reminders of the universality of growing up–moments of curiosity, self-discovery, and the early stirrings of relationships that are all part of every child's journey.

I did not experience much expression of love at home through words, kissing, or embracing. Instead, my siblings and I would kneel and worship our parents before leaving the house for school or any other place. We recited specific hymns to show our gratitude to them, and in return, they blessed us by placing their hands on our heads. However, I cannot recall them ever hugging or kissing us. Later in life, I came to recognise this as something I missed from my parents, though I now understand it was a cultural norm for them.

After Year 10 or tenth grade completion, my responsibilities at home changed. The tasks of assisting my father at the shop were gradually entrusted to my younger brothers, freeing me to focus on my studies and personal growth. This shift, however, also created some distance between my family and me. I struggled to find common ground with them, particularly as our age gaps and interests became more apparent.

My elder sister, only two years older than me, was a companion during my childhood, while with my younger siblings–two brothers and a sister ranging from four to eight years younger than me–I adopted a more dominant role as the eldest brother. This dynamic meant that while I cared for them, we lacked the camaraderie I shared with my elder sister.

My relationship with my father was also complex. At times, he would compare me to my elder sister, praising her qualities in ways that inadvertently made me feel inadequate. While his criticisms hurt, they also motivated me to strive harder, to prove my worth and set an example for my siblings. These moments, though painful, became catalysts for self-improvement and resilience in me.

One unfortunate incident involving my mother and younger brother remains etched in my memory. My mother, in a rush to get us ready for an event, grew increasingly frustrated when my brother refused to let her put his shoes on. She turned to me for assistance, hoping I could calm him down, but he continued to resist, crying uncontrollably. As the situation escalated, to my surprise, my mother's frustration shifted toward me. Unable to manage my brother, I found myself on the receiving end of her scolding, accompanied by a few quick hits. At the time, the incident felt profoundly unfair, leaving me hurt and confused. Looking back, this minor event stands out as a poignant reminder of the complexities of family dynamics—how stress and urgency can sometimes lead to misplaced emotions, even in loving family relationships.

The independence I was afforded, coupled with the guidance of my teachers, set the stage for everything that followed. My time at Kahawatta Primary School was not just about academic learning: it was a period of self-realisation, growth, and preparation for the future. It also gave me the tools and confidence to take on challenges, develop leadership qualities, and express myself in ways that would leave a lasting impact on me.

Through the highs and occasional awkwardness of childhood, I began to understand who I was and the person I wanted to become. These early years were a powerful blend of freedom, encouragement, and discovery that shaped the trajectory of my life, inspiring me to dream bigger and aim higher.

After completing my Year 10 examinations, my parents, recognising my growing maturity, granted me the freedom to make my own decisions, such as engaging in public events, choosing my friends, choosing my education and where I go. They allowed me to explore my interests and trusted me to seek their support when necessary. This newfound independence was exhilarating, opening opportunities for personal growth and exploration for me. I began to navigate life with a sense of autonomy that was both empowering and enlightening.

Sometimes the new independence came with some humourous moments, Many nights, I found myself returning home late, whether from visiting friends or attending social engagements. These journeys often involved walking approximately three kilometres from town to our home in complete darkness, a trek that took about thirty minutes. The stillness of the night amplified every sound, and my imagination sometimes turned the shadows into ominous figures. On one occasion, I unknowingly walked over a cow lying in the middle of the road, an event that startled us both! At other times, memories of my father's ghost stories sent me running through the darkness, my fear propelling me forward.

Learning at Pelmadulla Central College

After completing my primary school education, I faced a pivotal decision about where to continue my studies. Although there was a secondary school in Kahawatta, I chose to enrol in Pelmadulla Central College, a decision that would shape the next stage of my academic and personal growth. This choice, though unusual for a student from my area, reflected my desire to seek broader opportunities and challenge myself in a more dynamic environment.

I was fortunate to have the unwavering support of my parents, who respected my decision and provided everything I needed to make the transition into college. Despite the added logistical challenges, they ensured that I could attend Pelmadulla Central College with minimal obstacles.

Getting to school was far from easy. Each day, I walked about 2.5 kilometres to reach the bus stop in town. The bus itself was often overcrowded, with barely any room to stand, let alone sit comfortably. On those packed journeys, I learned patience, adaptability, and the resilience needed to overcome discomfort for the sake of pursuing my goals. These daily treks, though physically exhausting, became metaphors for my determination to push through challenges and reach greater heights.

My teenage years at Pelmadulla Central College were filled with growth, discovery, and a fair share of difficulties. As I immersed myself in the school community, I gravitated towards leadership roles, earning the respect of my peers and teachers. However, these responsibilities also came with moments of misunderstanding and adversity.

One such incident occurred during a farewell ceremony for a beloved chemistry teacher. I was tasked with giving a speech to honour him, and I decided to use a scientific analogy to express our admiration. Comparing the bond between sodium (Na^+) and chloride (Cl^-) in salt to the connection we students shared with our teacher, I sought to emphasise the strength and balance of that relationship together. I also praised the teacher for his humility and approachability, qualities that endeared him to us despite his status as a graduate teacher.

To my dismay, some graduate female teachers misinterpreted my words, believing I had implied that the teacher's graduate status was the exception rather than the rule. Although my intention had been to compliment his down-to-earth nature, my analogy unintentionally sparked offence. This incident taught me an early lesson about the power and potential pitfalls of communication, especially when addressing diverse audiences.

Another challenging moment came during my tenure as house captain. In keeping with tradition, I instructed the sports captain to organise practice sessions for our students during school hours. This was a widespread practice at the time, and the sports captain approached teachers to request that students be excused from class for these sessions. Unfortunately, a miscommunication occurred between the sports captain and one of the teachers, who was under the impression that I had directly ordered her to release the students.

This misunderstanding resulted in an unexpected summons to the principal's office. Without giving me an opportunity to explain myself, the principal accused me—albeit vaguely—of 'instructing' a teacher to send a student out of class during a lesson for sports training. Before I could respond, he struck me with a cane in front of the teacher. While the physical pain was brief, the emotional sting of such blatant injustice lingered far longer. I knew I had acted in good faith, adhering to established norms, yet I was punished without any inquiry or consideration.

This experience was a turning point in my understanding of authority and justice, leaving me questioning how easily misunderstandings could escalate and how crucial it was to ensure fairness in resolving conflicts. Though I endured most of the pain of this incident, it strengthened my resolve to stand up for what I believed was right and to approach leadership with greater empathy and clarity in the future.

My time at Pelmadulla Central College was a blend of triumphs and trials. It was a period that tested my resilience, sharpened my communication skills, and deepened my understanding of leadership.

While the challenges I faced sometimes felt overwhelming, they also provided invaluable lessons, as we have mentioned.

These experiences taught me that even well-intentioned actions can be misunderstood, and that miscommunication can lead to unintended consequences. They underscored the importance of listening, clarity, and fairness—principles that I carried forward in my personal and professional life.

Though the path was not always smooth, my years at Pelmadulla Central College laid the groundwork for my future endeavours in career and life. They strengthened my character, fuelled my ambition, and prepared me to navigate the complexities of life with determination and grace.

Music became for me another outlet for creativity and expression. Though I did not study music as a subject at school, I befriended the music teacher, who generously allowed me to practice the sitar in his office. This early connection to music sparked a lifelong passion, one that continues to bring joy and balance to my life. Later, I learned violin and guitar but never continued with any instrument besides those three.

During my time at Pelmadulla Central College, there was an occasion when my father came to meet the school principal to discuss my academic progress, though I cannot recall the exact reason for the meeting. Normally, it was my mother who handled school matters, but on this occasion, my father decided to come. I felt a bit anxious about the meeting, as I was present in the principal's office while they talked. I vividly remember the principal asking my father what I usually did at home and whether I spent much time on homework. To my surprise, my father replied that whenever he saw me, I would often tap on surfaces or tables, pretend to play drums, and frequently play the Dolakki, a traditional drumming instrument used in Indian and Sri Lankan classical music. Although his observation was accurate, I felt deeply embarrassed by my actions and had hoped he would emphasise how diligently I worked on my homework instead.

One particularly amusing incident occurred during Year 12. Some friends, impressed by my fluency in English, arranged an impromptu debate between me and a fellow student. Lacking preparation, I resorted to nonsensical phrases spoken with exaggerated confidence. To my surprise, my friends were convinced I had won the debate! This moment of humour highlighted the power of presentation and remains a fond memory of my school days.

While my academic journey at Pelmadulla Central College had its difficulties, my time in the Junior Cadet Corps at the college provided valuable lessons in discipline, leadership, and camaraderie. Starting as a lance corporal, I gradually rose through the ranks, eventually earning the position of a last sergeant, the sergeant being the highest rank attainable in the school cadet team.

One of the highlights of being in the Cadet Corps was the annual training camp and interschool competition at the Diyathalawa Army Camp, nestled in the breathtaking hill country of Sri Lanka. Renowned for its world-class facilities and scenic surroundings, the camp offered an unforgettable experience.

At Diyathalawa, we were subjected to rigorous training routines. Early mornings began with the blaring sound of bugles, followed by drills that demanded precision, teamwork, and endurance. The physical and mental challenges were intense, but they instilled a sense of discipline that would serve me well throughout my life.

Amid the seriousness of training, there were moments of levity that brought us closer as a team. One such occasion stands out vividly: During a camp event, I participated in a skit where I dressed as a woman, complete with makeup and traditional attire. With no females at the camp except for the wives of high-ranking officers, who occasionally attended special functions, my performance became a source of amusement and entertainment for the entire camp. The laughter and cheers of my fellow cadets were unforgettable, proving that even in a disciplined environment, there was room for humour and camaraderie.

Later, I joined the Senior Cadet Corps, where the training was even more intensive. This phase tested our endurance and sharpened our skills further, preparing us for greater challenges. The Diyathalawa camp remained a central part of this experience, offering a platform to push our limits and abilities while fostering an intense sense of brotherhood among cadets.

My time in the Cadet Corps taught me invaluable lessons that extended beyond the parade grounds. I learned the importance of discipline, the value of teamwork, and the strength that comes from perseverance. These experiences not only complemented my academic pursuits but also shaped my character, preparing me to face the challenges of life with courage and confidence.

One of the most defining incidents of my secondary school years unfolded when our male physics teacher was accused of leaking an examination paper to a female classmate. The act, perceived as favouritism and a breach of academic integrity, ignited outrage among the students. As one of the leaders in the student body, I felt compelled to join the protest organised by some students, believing it was the duty of students to hold those in authority accountable. However, the consequences of my actions were far-reaching. While our collective protest highlighted the issue, it also attracted the ire of the school administration. As the face of the movement, I bore the brunt of the backlash, and the principal imposed a harsh penalty: I was banned from holding any leadership positions at the school forever.

My secondary schooling was not solely about academics; it was also a time for exploring creative pursuits. I collaborated with a friend to produce a stage drama , successfully bringing it to life despite hurdles in gaining approval. This experience deepened my appreciation for the performing arts and taught me the value of persistence.

Determined to improve my English, I immersed myself in learning the language. Frequent visits to the library to read English newspapers, private tuition, and voracious reading of books like Dale Carnegie's 1936 bestselling book *How to Win Friends and Influence People* helped me build fluency and confidence. My efforts culminated in tutoring peers in English and chemistry for a small fee, further solidifying my skills and instilling a love for teaching.

Feeling unwelcome and misunderstood, I made the difficult decision to leave Pelmadulla Central College and pursue my education privately. Though this chapter of my education ended on a challenging note, it was not the end of my journey. Instead, it fuelled my resolve to succeed and proved to be a turning point in my life.

Private Study

Choosing to continue my studies privately required discipline, self-motivation, and an unwavering focus on my goals. Without the structure of a traditional school environment, I had to take responsibility for my own progress. The setbacks I faced at Pelmadulla only strengthened my determination to succeed, and I worked tirelessly to prepare for my future.

This perseverance paid off when I gained admission to the prestigious Colombo Medical School—a milestone that marked the culmination of years of hard work and resilience . It was a moment of triumph, proving that challenges could be transformed into stepping-stones for success.

CHAPTER 2
Rebellion, Revelry, and Revelations

Mischief and experimentation

My first encounter with alcohol came shortly after my Year 10 exam, marking a moment of youthful experimentation that, in hindsight, is both amusing and instructive. Feeling a mix of relief and excitement after completing the examinations, I decided to organise a celebratory party with a close-knit group of school friends. To keep our activities out of sight–and more importantly, out of mind–from my parents, we chose a small shed on our property as the drinking venue.

My parents, trusting the company I kept, had no reason to suspect any mischief. After all, my friends hailed from respectable families, and we were expected to spend the evening enjoying harmless, appropriate fun. What they did not know was that I had secretly procured a few bottles of homemade Sri Lankan toddy, a fermented coconut-based alcoholic drink that is deceptively sweet but potent in its effects.

The party began innocently enough, with cassava and other simple foods I had arranged to accompany our drinks. As the evening wore on and the toddy flowed, we grew more uninhibited. Laughter filled the air as we sang, joked, and indulged in the carefree revelry of youth. Some of my friends, unaccustomed to alcohol's effects, began to feel nauseous and started vomiting–a clear sign that we had overstepped our limits.

Despite the chaos, the evening ended without any major mishaps and, most importantly, without my parents discovering our escapade. Looking back, it was a light-hearted foray into adulthood, a moment of rebellion tempered by the camaraderie and innocence of youth.

Growing up, our shop stocked a variety of items, from daily essentials to Indigenous and Western remedies for common ailments. One such product, an herbal remedy called "Madana Modakaya," was particularly popular. It was touted as a cure for loss of appetite and other minor conditions, but it had an intriguing side effect: It contained marijuana, known to cause hallucinations when consumed.

Intrigued by the exaggerated claims surrounding the product, I decided to test it myself. I was sceptical that it could produce the effects people spoke of and voiced my doubts to my father, who knew of its effects as well. To my surprise, he did not dismiss my challenge; instead, he allowed me to conduct the experiment under his watchful eye.

I consumed a dose of the remedy, brimming with curiosity and a touch of bravado. It did not take long–about thirty minutes–before the effects kicked in. My head began to spin, and I was overcome with uncontrollable laughter. The world around me felt surreal, and in my altered state, I attempted to climb the walls of our home, much to the amusement of my father and the horror of my mother.

What started as a challenge quickly turned into an overwhelming experience. The disorientation and nausea that followed left me vowing never to try anything like that again. Though the episode was embarrassing at the time, it became a humorous anecdote in our family lore. My father chuckled at my misadventure while my mother scolded him for allowing me to go through with it. The "Madana Modakaya" incident was a stark reminder of the unpredictability of substances and the value of heeding caution. It was a playful yet profound example of how curiosity can lead to unexpected outcomes.

These experiences, while trivial, carried important lessons for me. My first encounter with alcohol taught me the importance of moderation and the consequences of overindulgence. It also underscored the sense of trust and freedom my parents had instilled in me, allowing me to explore boundaries within the safety net of their guidance. Both moments, though tinged with rebellion, were rooted in the safety of a loving and supportive environment. They were small steps on the path to self-discovery, shaping my understanding of responsibility, consequence, and the balance between curiosity and restraint .

A platform for expression and leadership

From an early age, I developed a close connection with the local temple and various community organisations, both of which became instrumental in shaping my confidence and leadership skills. The temple, a hub of spiritual and social life, offered me opportunities to participate in events and contribute to the community. During Vesak–a festival that celebrates the birth of the Buddha–and other significant celebrations, I was often invited to host events and fundraisers as the master of ceremonies (MC).

These occasions were more than mere formalities: they were platforms where I honed my skills in public speaking, poetry, and even singing. The experience of addressing an audience, often composed of elders and respected community members, taught me poise and the art of connecting with people through words and also ignited a passion for public speaking that would later play a significant role in my life.

One particularly memorable moment was my first public speech at the age of fourteen. It was at the wedding of a close friend's sister where I was asked to speak on behalf of the bridal party. Though nervous, I accepted the challenge, and as I delivered my speech, the warmth of the audience's reception filled me with pride and excitement. Their enthusiastic response affirmed my ability to articulate thoughts and emotions in a way that resonated with others. This moment became a turning point, solidifying my love for public speaking and setting the stage for future engagements.

These community events also exposed me to the broader dynamics of local politics and public gatherings. I realised that I thrived in these settings, engaging with leaders, voicing ideas, and learning the nuances of discourse and debate from an early age. This exposure laid the groundwork for my understanding of governance and societal structures, even as I began to develop my own opinions about justice and equality.

In 1971, when I was in Year 10, I encountered a more turbulent side of political activism. That year, a hartal (demonstration) was organised by students in support of the Marxist Janatha Vimukthi Peramuna (JVP) movement, which was gaining traction across the country. Unaware of the planned demonstration, I arrived at school expecting a normal day. However, one of my closest friends, who also happened to be the nephew of a teacher, insisted that I join the protest.

The demonstration was chaotic, with students marching on the roads in front of the school, shouting slogans and eventually throwing stones at passing government buses. It was not long before the police intervened, and the school principal worked to restore order on the campus. The school was shut down to prevent further incidents, and I left the protest with conflicting emotions–both intrigued by the movement and uneasy about the chaos it had caused.

Although I sympathised with some of the principles of the JVP, including their focus on injustice and inequality, my involvement remained superficial. I never attended their classes or fully embraced their ideology, a decision influenced by my parents' strict guidance.

My father had a quiet yet profound way of imparting wisdom. I remember discussing issues like caste discrimination, economic disparity, and social injustice with him, passionately advocating for change. However, instead of debating, he simply held up his hand and asked me to observe it. "Do all the fingers on your hand look the same?" he asked. I replied, "No." Then he said no more, letting the simplicity of his analogy sink in. His point was clear: differences in society, much like the differences in our hands, are natural and unavoidable, but harmony lies in how we work together despite them. This brief yet powerful lesson planted a seed of understanding in me that grew with time. While I admired the ideals of equality championed by Marxism, I came to realise the value of moderation, individual freedoms, and democratic principles.

As I matured, my views evolved. The revolutionary fervour of Marxism, which had once intrigued me, gave way to a more nuanced appreciation of democratic systems. I came to value the ability to debate, dissent, and collaborate within a framework of rights and laws. My father's wisdom, combined with my exposure to different perspectives through community engagement and school, helped shape this transition of viewpoint.

These experiences taught me the importance of standing for justice while respecting the complexity of society. They also underscored the power of communication, whether through a speech at a wedding, hosting an event, or engaging in political discourse, to influence minds and inspire change.

The opportunities I had to speak, lead, and engage with my community during these formative years were transformative, not only sharpening my skills but also broadening my understanding of people and the world around me. Whether addressing a festive crowd at the temple or grappling with the moral dilemmas of a political protest, these moments helped define the person I was becoming: someone who valued fairness, sought understanding, and believed in the power to bring about change.

Political connections

My father was deeply committed to his political ideals and was well-known as a staunch supporter of the United National Party (UNP), a party widely regarded as a bastion of gentlemen and ladies who upheld and promoted democratic values at that time. His dedication went beyond passive endorsement; he actively worked to strengthen the party's presence in our village. Organising meetings, inviting prominent politicians to address local concerns, and encouraging young people to align with the UNP were all part of his efforts. Through his leadership, he helped create a robust support base for the party, fostering a sense of unity and purpose among the villagers.

My father's political activities often turned our home into a hive of discussion and strategy. The excitement of these gatherings left an impression on me as well, exposing me to the nuances of leadership, organisation, and public discourse from an early age. I vividly recall the enthusiasm with which he would rally villagers, often emphasising the importance of participation in governance and community decision-making.

One of the most poignant memories from this period was the passing of Dudley Senanayake, a former Prime Minister of Sri Lanka and the leader of the UNP, who died from a heart ailment in 1973 at age sixty-one. His passing was a moment of profound sorrow, not only for my father but for the entire village. For my father, Senanayake represented the ideals of good governance, democracy, and service to the people.

In response to this loss, my father organised a Dhamma talk, inviting a respected Buddhist monk to honour Senanayake's memory. It was a deeply moving event, and I felt privileged to assist him in making the arrangements for the service. Together, we ensured that the gathering was a meaningful tribute, blending spirituality with the values that Senanayake had embodied. The event left a lasting impact on me, further strengthening my appreciation for the intersection of community, politics, and culture.

Growing up in this politically charged environment, it was almost inevitable that I would develop an interest in politics: the debates, discussions, and community-building efforts I witnessed at home shaped my early understanding of political philosophy. My father's example, coupled with the principles of the UNP, inspired me to take an active role in the UNP.

As a teenager, I began speaking at public gatherings in support of UNP candidates. Despite my youth, I had a natural ability to connect with people through speech. One of my most significant political connections during this time was with the late Gamini Athukorala, a young UNP organiser in the neighbouring Nivithigala electorate who later became a deputy minister.

Athukorala recognised my potential and invited me to speak at his political events. These opportunities were both thrilling and humbling, as I stood before crowds much older and more experienced than myself. With every speech about the candidates, my confidence grew, and so did my understanding of the power of words to inspire and influence.

My relationship with Athukorala extended beyond politics to where he became a trusted mentor and later played a significant role in my personal life, serving as one of the witnesses at my wedding. His support during key moments was invaluable, and I remain grateful for the opportunities he provided.

Looking back, my father's dedication to the UNP and his active role in the village were more than just political acts. They were lessons in leadership, commitment, and the importance of community. Through his example, I learned that politics was not merely about power or ambition but about serving others and striving for the greater good.

These experiences laid the foundation for my early engagement in public life, teaching me the value of perseverance, collaboration, and the ability to articulate a vision. Whether organising a village meeting or addressing a crowd from a political stage, the lessons I absorbed during these formative years have stayed with me, guiding my journey and shaping my aspirations.

During this period of self-discovery, I was also captivated by stories of great lawyers like G.G. Ponnambalam who was the main defence lawyer in one of the late Sri Lankan prime minister's assassination trial in and around 1959. Their ability to craft compelling arguments and command respect in courtrooms fascinated me. Inspired by their eloquence and intellectual prowess, I briefly aspired to pursue a career in law, even researching the quickest path to becoming a lawyer, learning that admission to law college could follow successful completion of the GCE O/L examinations. However, this ambition, while intriguing, did not endure for long, as my interests shifted towards other pursuits.

Involvement in extracurricular activities

As my academic journey progressed and I gained admission to medical school, my involvement in social and political activities naturally waned. My focus shifted entirely to my studies and preparing for the challenges ahead.

However, my relationship with Buddhism, cultivated by my mother's devout practices, remained a source of inner peace to me. As a child, I regularly observed Sil on Poya days, practiced meditation, and sought guidance from monks for my path ahead. While this connection faded during my school years, it was later reignited after I moved to Perth in Western Australia, offering me a spiritual anchor amidst life's challenges.

These experiences–navigating independence, overcoming family tensions, exploring creative outlets, and embracing spirituality–shaped the foundation of my adult life. They taught me resilience, adaptability, and the importance of pursuing passions alongside responsibilities. Each step in growth brought me closer to understanding who I was and the values I wanted to carry forward in career and life, laying the groundwork for the person I would eventually become.

One of the pivotal influences in my journey to mastering English came from Ms. Concy, a kind and dedicated young teacher at the Kahawatta Convent. Her real name, I believe, was Constance, but to us, she was simply Ms. Concy, a figure of grace and encouragement. Her lessons went far beyond grammar and vocabulary; she instilled in us the confidence to express ourselves fluently, emphasising the transformative power of language.

Ms. Concy had a remarkable way of connecting with her students, being patient yet firm, and her passion for teaching was evident in every session. During school holidays, she would open her home to students for additional tuition, offering us an opportunity to refine our skills in a relaxed yet focused environment. It was through her unwavering support that my command of the English language began to take shape, laying a foundation that would prove invaluable in the years to come.

When I began my Advanced Level studies, a few of my friends suggested that I share what I had learned by teaching English to others. Encouraged by their faith in my abilities, I started an English tuition class at the same convent where Ms. Concy had once taught me. Most of my students were my classmates or peers from Pelmadulla Central College.

Teaching was both a rewarding and enlightening experience, only allowing me to give back by helping others improve their skills, but also deepening my own understanding of the language. The act of explaining concepts to others solidified my knowledge of English, while the small fees my friends paid for the lessons gave me a sense of independence. It was my first taste of being a mentor and a leader, roles that I grew to cherish and embrace.

Friendships and pursuing a new path

Throughout this period of education, I was fortunate to have the steadfast support of two close friends from my early school days, Nanda and Kosala. Both were the sons of my pre-primary teacher Mrs Wicramaratne, and our bond, formed during childhood, carried us through the challenges of growing up.

Although our paths eventually diverged after Year 10, the subtle contributions they made to my life continued to resonate. Their friendship taught me the value of loyalty and shared aspirations. Even as I began gravitating towards friends with influence or social standing and the values that I admired–a trait that has persisted to this day–I always appreciated the grounding presence of Nanda and Kosala and a handful of friends in my formative years.

Sadly, as I forged my own path, I could not help but feel that I had disappointed my father by not continuing to work at the family shop. He had envisioned a future where I would take over the business and carry on his legacy within the village. But I felt that my destiny lay elsewhere, far beyond the boundaries of our small community.

The decision to pursue a different path of career was not an easy one, but it was necessary. I did not want to confine myself to the familiar rhythms of village life: I yearned to explore, learn, and grow. While this choice may have caused my father some initial disappointment, I believe that, in time, he came to admire the person I had become and felt pride in my accomplishments.

Reflecting on my journey, from the humble beginnings in Polwatta to the hallowed halls of Colombo Medical School, I see a tapestry woven with challenges, triumphs, and invaluable lessons. It was a path far from straightforward, marked by moments of self-doubt, resilience, and growth.

One of the key lessons I learned early in life was the profound value of giving to others. Whether it was sharing my knowledge or offering help, I discovered that the act of teaching or guiding others enriched me in ways I had not anticipated. By educating others, I gained exponentially: my own understanding deepened, my confidence soared, and my capacity to connect with people grew stronger. This principle of teaching became a cornerstone of my personal and professional philosophy, one that I would carry throughout my life.

Every experience, from the confidence I gained through public speaking to the discipline instilled by the Cadet Corps, played a role in shaping my character. The relationships I built, the values I embraced, and the skills I developed became the foundation upon which my future success was built.

For these transformative years, I am profoundly grateful to my parents and teachers. Their guidance–whether deliberate or inadvertent–set me on a course that would define my life. My mother's unwavering devotion, my father's discipline and political engagement, and the encouragement of mentors like Ms. Concy all left indelible marks on my journey.

The road I have travelled thus far has taught me that success is not simply about reaching a destination but about embracing the lessons learned along the way. Every obstacle overcome, every skill learned, and every connection made was a step towards becoming the person I aspired to be.

As I reached the threshold of Colombo Medical School, the excitement of what lay ahead was palpable. The journey that had brought me to this point in my life and career was only the beginning, a prelude to a story yet to unfold. The next chapter of my life promised new challenges, opportunities, and experiences, the start of a new adventure, one that would push me to grow further and define my place in the world.

CHAPTER 3
Medical School and Medical Career in Sri Lanka

Entering medical school was a transformative chapter in my life, a journey that demanded focus, resilience, and the ability to adapt to a new and challenging environment. I approached it with the seriousness it deserved, recognising the privilege and responsibility that came with pursuing a career in medicine.

In the early part of my education, I stayed with one of my mother's cousins in Wellampitiya, a bustling suburb of Colombo. My daily commute to the Colombo Medical Faculty involved taking the Route 166 bus, and it quickly became part of my routine. The journey was surprisingly pleasant, often shared with cheerful schoolchildren heading to the many prestigious schools near the medical faculty. Their lively chatter and laughter brought a sense of energy to the mornings, making the commute an enjoyable start to the day. My hosts–my uncle and aunt–were incredibly kind and supportive, ensuring I felt at home during this important transition in my life.

Before entering medical school, I had heard unsettling stories about ragging, a practice involving senior students subjecting newcomers to humiliating or intimidating behaviour. It was a tradition I disliked on principle, as it served no purpose other than perpetuating a cycle of power and fear.

Thankfully, the ragging in medical school was not as severe as I had anticipated. Most of my seniors were respectful and maintained the dignity expected in a professional institution. However, there was one incident that remains etched in my memory.

A senior approached me one day and casually asked, "What school are you from?" I replied with pride, "Pelmadulla Central College." His reaction was immediate and mockingly loud, ensuring that everyone around could hear. "Look at this guy," he exclaimed, dripping with sarcasm, "he's from Pelmadulla Central College," as though it were a name worthy of scorn. The implication was clear: My school, though respectable, did not carry the prestige of elite Colombo schools, and the senior's ridicule was intended to emphasise that difference.

At that moment, I realised how some people use status to belittle others, but I refused to let it affect me. I remained composed during this interaction, aware that no matter what I said, the goal was to find fault and embarrass me.

The experience of being mocked for my school, though unpleasant, only strengthened my resolve. It reminded me that excellence is not defined by where you come from but by the effort and commitment you bring to your pursuits. However, for reasons I cannot fully explain, I was mostly left alone from mischief. Whether it was my quiet determination or the way I carried myself, I avoided becoming a target. But I also noticed that others were not as fortunate because some of my peers were bullied, enduring unkind remarks or tasks designed to humiliate them.

This initial period in medical school, though humbling, set the tone for the journey ahead, a reminder that resilience and self-assurance are as vital as knowledge and skill. Looking back, I am grateful for these experiences, as they taught me to stand firm in the face of judgment and to focus on what truly mattered: the path I was carving for myself.

After my first year of medical school, I moved to Kohuwala, a quiet suburb conveniently located near my clinical placement at Colombo South General Hospital. This change in residence brought me closer to the hands-on training that was integral to my studies. While I attended clinical sessions at the hospital, my lectures were held at the Medical Faculty on Kings Road, Punchi Borella, a routine that required balancing travel with the demands of rigorous coursework.

The move to Kohuwala marked the start of a more immersive phase of my education. It was in these years that I had the privilege of being taught by some of the most eminent figures in Sri Lankan medicine. Professors Colvin Goonaratna and Carlo Fonseka were among the brilliant minds who shaped my understanding of the field. Occasionally, we were graced by lectures from luminaries such as Professors Priyani Soysa and Lamabadusooriya, whose insights left lasting impressions on me. Alongside these remarkable professors, there were countless other tutors and lecturers whose dedication and expertise elevated our learning experience.

My thirst for knowledge often led me beyond the classroom to where I spent hours in the libraries of the British Council and the American Embassy, delving into books, journals, and resources that expanded my perspective and deepened my understanding of medicine. These libraries were sanctuaries of learning, offering an atmosphere of quiet focus that complemented the intensity of medical school.

Life at Kohuwala

During this time, my closest companion was Ramya Padithrathna, one of my best mates, who shared many of my interests and became a trusted confidant. We spent countless hours discussing life, studies, and everything in between. One day, inspired by a desire to add a bit of flair to our routines, I suggested we take ballroom dancing classes together. Ramya, however, was not convinced so I decided to attend the classes alone.

The lessons were held in Wellawatta, and my instructor was Ms. Rodrigo, a seasoned teacher with a commanding presence. While I was excited to learn, I must admit that I had imagined myself dancing with a slim, graceful partner, as seen in movies. Instead, Ms. Rodrigo, who was twice my size and full of energy, became my partner. Though she was an excellent teacher, our sessions felt less like a waltz and more like an exercise in endurance, as she pushed and pulled me across the dance floor.

After a few lessons, I decided to stop, feeling that the experience did not meet my expectations. However, my interest in ballroom dancing never faded, as later, I returned to it and found immense joy in learning the graceful movements and rhythms of the dance. It became a pastime that brought balance and excitement to my life, proving that early disappointments need not define the pursuit of a passion.

Romance during medical school, much like in my earlier years, was fleeting. If a girl expressed interest in me, I inexplicably lost interest and moved on. It was a pattern I did not fully understand at the time, but one that remained consistent throughout this phase of my life.

Back then, my slim physique was not particularly attractive, especially to the opposite sex. Eager to improve my appearance, I tried experimenting with my style and began wearing photochromic glasses, even though I did not need them, hoping they would add a touch of sophistication to me. I also frequented a trendy hairdresser in Wellawatta, attempting to give my hairstyle a more fashionable edge. Despite my efforts, none of these changes seemed to make a significant difference in my attractiveness to women. Disheartened, I eventually gave up on these pursuits, accepting myself as I was.

Life at the Kohuwala boarding house was an experience of its own, outside of medical school and fledging social life. The food was a constant source of frustration, as meals often consisted of kirihodi or hodda, thin gravies that were watery and tasteless. The house was crowded, with numerous people sharing the space, and after some time, another medical student moved into my room, which we then shared.

One day, my roommate and I decided to send a message to the boarding mistress about the state of the meals. After finishing a portion of hodda (thin gravy), scraping the bottom of the container where the concentrated flavours lingered, we added more water to the remaining gravy to make it looks more watery and less tasteful and placed it back on the table. The diluted, flavourless result was our way of highlighting the food problem. Whether the message was received or not, it brought a moment of humour to an otherwise monotonous dining routine.

Those years were a blend of intensity and experimentation. Balancing the rigours of medical school with fleeting attempts at hobbies, personal growth, and managing the challenges of boarding life shaped my resilience and adaptability. While my experiments with dancing, music, and style may not have been long-lasting at first, they later evolved into meaningful passions, particularly ballroom dancing, which became a source of joy and expression.

Looking back, even the frustrations of watered-down hodda and the missteps in early hobby pursuits were part of a larger tapestry. They were moments that taught me to laugh at myself, find joy in the unexpected, and focus on what truly mattered.

Memorable moments in medical school

My time at medical school was not just about mastering the sciences: it was a period rich with experiences that tested my skills, broadened my horizons, and occasionally challenged my composure. Among these, a few incidents remain etched in my memory, offering lessons in responsibility, humility, and the unpredictability of life.

During my Gynaecology and Obstetrics placement, we were required to perform several deliveries as part of our clinical training, and it was during one such delivery that I encountered an event that I still vividly recall. The delivery was progressing as expected, and I performed an episiotomy, a surgical incision made at the opening of the vagina to aid the baby's birth. After the delivery, I packed the vaginal area with swabs to stem the bleeding and make the site of the incision clear for suturing. Exhausted after a long day, I returned home that night, but as I lay in bed, a horrifying realisation struck me: I had forgotten to remove the vaginal pack before leaving.

Panic set in immediately, as the potential consequences of such a mistake raced through my mind. Without wasting a moment, I hurried back to the hospital–it must have been around 11 p.m.–to address the situation. When I reached the ward, I approached the mother, careful not to alarm her. She seemed calm and had no complaints, which was a relief. Still, I needed to ensure that the pack was removed without raising unnecessary concerns. I told her I needed to conduct a quick examination, and during this process, I discreetly removed the forgotten pack. The weight of anxiety lifted as I left the hospital that night, but the incident served as a powerful reminder of the importance of vigilance and thoroughness in medical practice.

Beyond the hospital walls, I sought opportunities to hone my practical clinical skills. Together with some of my batchmates, I joined the Red Cross First-Aid crew, which provided medical aid at various community events. It was a chance to step out of the academic setting and engage directly with people in need, putting our training into action.

One memorable experience was serving at a First-Aid post on Sri Pada (Adam's Peak) during the pilgrimage season. Thousands of devotees climbed the sacred mountain, and it was our job to attend to those who fell ill or injured along the way. On one occasion, a young woman approached me complaining of chest pain, a potentially serious symptom. Before I could assess her condition, she asked, "Are you the doctor?" With confidence, I replied, "Yes." Her response, however, was not what I expected. Instead of following my advice, she looked at me, a lean and slender figure at the time, and said, "You should take some vitamins!" In her mind, the vitamins might help me grow physically stronger, but her comment was a humorous reminder of how appearances can influence perceptions, even in serious situations. Although my ego took a slight hit, I carried on with my duties, grateful for the hands-on experience and the opportunity to serve.

Among the many extracurricular activities that enriched my time in medical school, one stands out as a deeply fulfilling moment. I had the extraordinary opportunity to sing alongside Victor Ratnayake, one of Sri Lanka's most celebrated vocalists, as part of a radio program designed to showcase novice singers. I had sung on numerous occasions before and even won singing competitions. However, this was a very special event.

The format was simple: The iconic singer would perform one of his songs, followed by the novice singing one of the original singers' songs. For my audition, I selected the Buddhist devotional song, "Dewuram

Vehere Himi Weda Siti Samaye," a timeless piece that resonated with spirituality and grace.

The experience of standing on stage with Victor Ratnayake was surreal. His presence was commanding yet encouraging, and I was filled with a mix of nerves and excitement as I sang. When the program aired, I was overwhelmed by the response, as letters and cards poured in from listeners, filled with kind words and congratulations. These messages, with their warmth and encouragement, remain among my most treasured memories.

These moments, rushing back to the hospital to correct a mistake, tending to pilgrims on Sri Pada, and singing alongside a musical legend, were as valuable to my development as a doctor as the hours spent in lectures or clinical placements. They taught me lessons that went beyond medicine: the importance of responsibility, the value of humility, and the joy of embracing unexpected opportunities.

As I reflect on these experiences, I am reminded that life is not solely defined by the profession we choose but also by the richness of the journey, the people we meet, and the moments that shape us along the way. These memories remain vivid, not just for the lessons they imparted but for the way they added depth and meaning to my time in medical school.

More adventures

My life at medical school was filled with small adventures and incidents that brought laughter, lessons, and, occasionally, a dose of humility. One such memory involved a trip to the Ceylinco Building to collect an advertisement for the student journal, that turned into an unexpectedly comical episode. Accompanied by my close friends Ramya and Rupa, I headed to the Ceylinco Building, a towering landmark in

Colombo. We were tasked with collecting an advertisement from a pharmaceutical company, a straightforward task.

As we entered this very tall multi-story building, we encountered something we had never seen before: escalators. The gleaming, moving stairs stood before us, and for a moment, we were mesmerised. With no one else around to guide us, we hesitated, unsure which escalator was meant to take us up. In our confusion, we stepped onto the wrong one- the escalator that was bringing people down instead of up. Initially, we did not realise our mistake, but as we found ourselves moving in the opposite direction of our intended destination, the realisation dawned on us. Instead of stepping off and choosing the correct escalator, we decided to challenge ourselves. With laughter echoing in the empty lobby, we raced upward against the downward motion of the escalator, taking double steps to reach the next floor. When we finally reached the top, we were breathless and could not stop laughing at our own silliness. It was a moment of light-hearted joy, a reminder that even the simplest tasks can become unforgettable adventures when shared with good friends.

While I did not have a serious romantic relationship during medical school, there was one brief connection with a junior female student. Our interactions and conversations mutually made us happy but fleeting, as she soon decided to pursue her medical studies overseas. When it was time for her to leave, my ever-encouraging friend Ramya suggested we go to the airport to bid her farewell. Ramya, resourceful as always, arranged to borrow his uncle's motorbike, a treasured possession belonging to none other than Vijaya Kumaratunga, a well-known Sri Lankan actor and political figure.

The journey to the airport was uneventful, and we managed to say our goodbyes to our friend. However, the return trip turned into an adventure we had not anticipated. Somewhere near Ja-Ela, a car traveling in front of us suddenly made an abrupt turn without signalling. Unable to react in time, we collided and were thrown off the motorbike.

Though the injuries we sustained were non-fatal, they were significant enough to cause us pain and concern; the motorbike, too, was damaged. Fortunately, the driver of the car was a decent man who helped us get to the nearest doctor's private clinic. To our surprise, the doctor, after hearing that our injuries were accident-related, refused to provide even basic first aid. He suggested instead that we go to the general hospital, leaving us to fend for ourselves to get there safely.

Despite our injuries, we mustered the strength to ride the damaged motorbike to the hospital, where we received the treatment we needed and were discharged the same day. The physical pain was manageable, but the incident left us shaken. What worried us most, however, was the condition of the motorbike. Knowing it was his uncle's first vehicle, Ramya was especially concerned about the repairs. Thankfully, his uncle was understanding and managed to get the bike repaired at his own cost. For two students living on limited means, this outcome was a huge relief.

Looking back, these events were more than just anecdotes; they were reminders of the resilience and resourcefulness we cultivated during our medical school years. Whether it was laughing at our own naivety on an escalator or finding the courage to handle a minor accident with limited resources, each experience added to the tapestry of our journey.

They also underscored the importance of friendship and support. In every misstep or challenge, the presence of close friends like Ramya made all the difference. These moments, however small or inconvenient they seemed at the time, became cherished memories that brought humour, strength, and perspective to our lives.

A new avenue: learning acupuncture

After completing my first year of medical studies, I decided to broaden my horizons by enrolling in a course on acupuncture, a field that fascinated me for its holistic approach to healing. The course was conducted by the world-renowned expert, Professor Anton Jayasuriya, whose reputation as a pioneer in acupuncture was matched only by his passion for teaching.

Jayasuriya operated an acupuncture clinic within the Colombo South General Hospital and ran an international education institute for acupuncture, making him an integral figure in bridging traditional and modern medical practices in Sri Lanka. His weekly lectures on acupuncture practices were held in the evenings at the Royal College Auditorium in Colombo. The institution he founded later evolved into the Open International University of Complementary Medicine, receiving support from the then-President of Sri Lanka, the late Mr. J.R. Jayewardene. However, the organisation faced significant criticism from certain higher education and medical establishments within Sri Lanka due to its unconventional practices and growing international recognition and popularity.

The course brought together a diverse group of students: doctors, medical students, and Ayurvedic physicians all united by a shared curiosity about acupuncture. Remarkably, there was no hierarchy or discrimination in the classroom among anyone, as Jayasuriya treated everyone as equals, fostering an inclusive and respectful learning environment.

His lectures were nothing short of inspiring. Jayasuriya had a unique ability to simplify complex concepts, making acupuncture accessible to anyone, regardless of their prior medical knowledge. His deep understanding of human anatomy and physiology, coupled with his mastery of acupuncture, allowed him to convey the subject in a way that was both engaging and educational.

What truly set him apart, however, was his humour and charisma, as his lectures were not just lessons in medicine but performances that kept the audience captivated. He interwove anecdotes, real-life examples, and moments of levity into his teachings, transforming the study of acupuncture into a joyful and memorable experience for his students.

Under Jayasuriya's guidance, I gained not only theoretical knowledge but also a deeper appreciation for the art and science of acupuncture. His insights illuminated how traditional practices could complement modern medicine, providing a more comprehensive approach to patient care, particularly in the management of some chronic pain and musculo-skeletal disorders, which I shared with my colleagues and incorporated into my own clinical practice to enhance patient outcomes.

But beyond the technical aspects, his lectures instilled in me a sense of curiosity and a willingness to explore alternative medical practices. The experience was a reminder that learning is not confined to textbooks and classrooms but thrives in the exchange of ideas and the sharing of wisdom across disciplines.

Looking back, I realise how fortunate I was to have been taught by someone of Professor Jayasuriya's calibre. His influence extended beyond the subject of acupuncture and exemplified what it meant to be a teacher: someone who not only imparts knowledge but also inspires a love for learning.

This experience enriched my medical education, adding a layer of depth and diversity that continues to shape my perspective on healthcare. It was a testament to the power of great teaching and the impact of a passionate mentor which I shared with many others later in life in Australia through my employment and my own educational establishments.

Completing the acupuncture course under the mentorship of Professor Jayasuriya was a transformative experience. Armed with the knowledge and skills I had gained, I began treating patients privately, focusing on those within my circle of acquaintances. This hands-on experience was invaluable because it allowed me to hone my clinical skills, build confidence, and take on professional responsibility in patient management. These early interactions gave me a sense of purpose and reinforced my belief in the therapeutic potential of acupuncture.

During this time, acupuncture gained significant momentum in Sri Lanka due to Jayasuriya's influence. His clinic at the Colombo South General Hospital (CSGH) became a hub of activity, attracting not only local students but also many foreign delegates and medical professionals, including many from China, the birthplace of acupuncture. Professor Jayasuriya's reputation extended everywhere, and his mastery of the subject was on full display during surgical procedures conducted under acupuncture anaesthesia at CSGH. Watching these surgeries was a remarkable experience, one that showcased the clinical potential of acupuncture in the modern medical landscape. These procedures were a testament to the depth of Jayasuriya's knowledge and his commitment to advancing the field.

Jayasuriya's photographic memory was another aspect of his brilliance, as he could recall intricate details about acupuncture points, their applications, and even complex case histories with astonishing accuracy. This remarkable ability added an extra layer of awe and respect to the learning process under him, making his lectures and clinical demonstrations even more impactful.

As the final acupuncture examination approached, a few of us decided to have a group study session to review the material and solidify our understanding. The group included Ramya, Rupa, Sarath A., and me. While discussing acupuncture points and their locations, we were all deeply engrossed, except for Sarath A., who fell asleep mid-session.

To inject some humour into the situation, I decided to wake him up in an unconventional way. Picking up an acupuncture needle, I carefully inserted it into the resuscitation point located just below the nose, known in acupuncture for its sensitivity and use in reviving unconscious patients. Sarath's reaction was instantaneous; he panicked and woke up in a state of confusion, shouting for us to remove the needle. We quickly obliged, removing the needle amid fits of laughter. Sarath, needless to say, stayed awake for the rest of the session!

The incident became an enduring memory of our time together, blending the seriousness of our studies with the camaraderie and humour that lightened the journey.

These experiences, whether funny or educational, not only deepened my understanding of acupuncture but also enriched my overall medical education. Treating patients privately taught me responsibility, while witnessing acupuncture's application in surgery, expanded my perspective on integrative medicine. The camaraderie with my peers and the inspiration drawn from Jayasuriya's brilliance added layers of depth and meaning to this chapter of my life. His guidance, mentorship, and encouragement were pivotal in enabling me to successfully complete my PhD, which focused on managing chronic musculoskeletal disorders using acupuncture in an outpatient setting.

Looking back, I am profoundly grateful for these moments, as they reinforced the importance of curiosity, hands-on learning, and the value of humour and friendship in navigating the challenges of medical training. Acupuncture became more than just a course; it became a lens through which I could view the possibility of combining ancient wisdom with modern medical practices.

Internship in Badulla

After completing my medical studies, I was thrilled to receive my first appointment as an intern at Badulla General Hospital. This was a placement I had specifically requested, eager to begin my professional journey amidst the breathtaking beauty of Sri Lanka's hill country. Badulla, surrounded by lush tea plantations and misty mountains, offered not just an ideal environment for reflection and growth but also the promise of a new, successful chapter in my life.

From the moment I joined the hospital, I was met with kindness and support from all the consultants. Among them, two consultants who left an indelible mark on my memory and career: Dr B.J.C. Perera, a highly skilled paediatrician and an exceptional leader and Dr C De Silva , a kind general physician.

Dr. Perera's bedside manner was exemplary, for he approached every patient with a mix of empathy, clinical precision, and calm reassurance that put both patients and staff at ease. Observing his patient interactions was like witnessing the art of medicine in motion. Dr. Perera combined technical expertise with a human touch that was deeply inspiring.

Beyond his clinical skills, Dr. Perera's leadership qualities were equally striking. During ward rounds, he fostered an environment of learning and growth, encouraging interns like me to ask questions and engage in meaningful discussions with him. It was during one such ward round that he planted a seed of ambition in my mind. Noticing my curiosity and thoughtful questions during rounds, he spoke to me about the importance of pursuing higher education. His words resonated deeply, sparking a motivation that would quietly grow within me for years to come.

Years later, when I decided to pursue a Doctor of Medicine (MD) degree at IUHS, a university in St. Kitts, West Indies, I remembered Dr. Perera's encouragement and reached out to him, hoping he would write me a letter of reference. Admittedly, I was unsure whether he would even recall me after all those years, but I decided to try. To my surprise and delight, Dr. Perera responded promptly to my request, vividly remembering me in his words. What struck me most was his mention of the photochromic glasses I had worn during my internship, a small detail that showed the depth of his attentiveness. He agreed without hesitation to write me the reference letter, a gesture that spoke volumes about his generosity and belief in his students. That letter was instrumental in securing my admission to the MD program, and our correspondence did not end there. Over the years, we continued to stay in touch, exchanging updates and sharing moments of connection that reinforced the profound impact he had on my life.

Looking back, my time in Badulla was more than just an internship; it was a turning point that laid the foundation for my aspirations in medicine and life. Dr. Perera's encouragement and mentorship were pivotal, instilling in me the confidence to pursue opportunities I might not have otherwise considered.

His leadership style, which balanced authority with approachability, became a model I sought to emulate in my own career. The way he nurtured curiosity and ambition in young doctors like me was a reminder of the transformative power of a great mentor in a person's life.

The enriching experiences at Badulla General Hospital, against the backdrop of the hill country's serene beauty, made my internship a period of immense personal and professional growth. It was here that I began to see the wider possibilities in medicine, realising that a career in healthcare could be as much about education and leadership as it was about clinical practice.

This chapter of my life reinforced an essential lesson: the value of encouragement. Whether it is a thoughtful word during a ward round or a letter of reference written years later, the belief someone shows in you can be a catalyst for growth, inspiring you to reach heights you never imagined possible.

A new chapter in Badalkumbura

Life in Badulla had been fulfilling, and as I approached the end of my internship, I began to think about the next step in my medical journey. It was then that I learned about a vacancy at a district hospital in Badalkumbura, a quiet suburb nestled between Badulla and Monaragala. The rural location meant there was not much competition for the position, as it was not the first choice for many doctors. But for me, the opportunity felt like a perfect fit.

I saw Badalkumbura not as a remote posting but as a chance to grow in my skills. The idea of managing a hospital single-handedly was both exciting and daunting, promising invaluable experience, a chance to meet new people, and the opportunity to earn money while enjoying the serenity of rural life.

At Badalkumbura Hospital, I was entrusted with significant responsibilities. The hospital had three inpatient wards: male, female, and maternity, as well as an outpatient department (OPD). While the wards were often full, the OPD saw a more manageable flow of patients, which allowed me to focus on the more critical cases.

In addition to providing medical care, I was also responsible for hospital administration, managing staff, and ensuring the smooth running of daily operations. The hospital's infrastructure included a newly built administrative and OPD block, making it a more modern facility compared to many rural hospitals.

The hospital's team of about twenty staff members, mostly locals, was a mix of warmth and dedication. Periodically, a United Nations medical officer would join on a contractual basis, adding a touch of global connection to this otherwise local institution and filling the acute shortage of doctors in the rural hospitals.

The Department of Health provided a doctor's residence that became my home once I arrived. The accommodation was comfortable, offering me a much-needed retreat after long days at the hospital. The residence also added to the charm of my stay, making life in Badalkumbura not only manageable but genuinely enjoyable.

One of the most memorable aspects of my time in Badalkumbura was the warm welcome from the community. My predecessor introduced me to a local family who ran a thriving retail business in the area and had a tradition of taking care of the doctors who came to serve at the hospital. They extended their hospitality to me with open arms.

Mr. and Mrs. Gunasekara, kind and generous, treated me as if I were part of their family, often inviting me to their home for dinners where I enjoyed delicious meals and heartfelt conversations. Their two sons, Sarath and Sumith, became close friends of mine. Respectful and thoughtful, they were always willing to lend a hand whenever I needed help. Whether it was arranging transportation, assisting with local matters, or simply offering companionship, their support made my time in Badalkumbura even more enriching.

Managing Badalkumbura

Working in Badalkumbura was a defining period in my early medical career. Managing multiple wards, interacting with diverse patients, and navigating the administrative aspects of running a hospital all provided invaluable experience. The quiet outpatient department allowed me to dedicate more time to complex cases and build deeper connections with my patients and staff.

The combination of professional responsibility, a supportive community, and the tranquillity of rural life gave me the perfect environment to learn, grow, and thrive. It was a chapter filled with challenges, opportunities, and relationships that left a lasting impact on my journey.

Badalkumbura, with its limited facilities and public offices, presented an unexpected advantage as well: The opportunity to meet and connect with key figures in the community on a personal level. In the absence of the hustle and anonymity of a larger town, I was able to form meaningful relationships with the people who kept the town running.

Among the most memorable of these connections was my friendship with Mr. Gunawardana, the branch manager of the Bank of Ceylon in Badalkumbura. During my first visit to the bank, he greeted me warmly and assisted me in setting up the accounts I needed. What stood out in our interaction was his efficiency and kindness. He completed everything I required on the very same day, a gesture that laid the foundation for a lifelong friendship.

Though Mr. Gunawardana was older than me, his youthful spirit made him an easy companion, and our friendship quickly grew beyond professional interactions. He often visited me at my residence, and on several occasions, he stayed overnight, adding to the camaraderie that had developed. Our evenings together were lively, often filled with conversations, laughter, and the occasional gathering. Whenever I hosted get-togethers and parties, Mr. Gunawardana was a regular guest, bringing warmth and humour to the occasion.

Over time, he introduced me to his wife and two children, and during school holidays, they would come to spend a few days with me in Badalkumbura. Those moments were unforgettable, filled with shared meals, stories, and the kind of connection that transcends time.

Even after I moved on from Badalkumbura, our friendship endured. We stayed in touch, and for thirty years, until his passing, he remained a cherished friend. His openness, generosity, and zest for life left a lasting impression on me, reminding me of the richness of human connections that can emerge in the most unexpected places (like in a bank).

During my time in Badalkumbura, I also formed a lifelong friendship with Mr. Weerakoon, the assistant government agent of the area. As he did not have an official residence there, I was fortunate to offer him accommodations at my residence. This arrangement not only made us housemates but also fostered a deep and enduring friendship. To this day, he remains a trusted and loyal friend. Whenever I visit Sri Lanka, I make it a point to meet him, and we often reminisce about our time in Badalkumbura. Mr. Weerakoon continues to express heartfelt gratitude for my small gesture of hospitality. After his time in Badalkumbura, he advanced in his career to become the additional government agent in Galle before retiring from public service.

In a place like Badalkumbura, where resources were limited, relationships like the one I had with Mr. Gunawardana and Mr. Weerakoon added depth and meaning to everyday life. They were reminders that even in the simplest settings, bonds of friendship and shared humanity have the power to transform a professional posting into a profoundly personal and fulfilling experience.

Struggles in Badalkumbura

Of course, life in Badalkumbura had its challenges, particularly when it came to managing the hospital staff. Among them were a few individuals whose behaviour posed unique problems but also offered valuable lessons in leadership and patience to me.

Early in my tenure, I noticed a peculiar issue: The surgical spirit/alcohol allocated to the wards would disappear unusually quickly, and it did not take long to uncover the culprits. Two staff members had developed the dangerous habit of consuming the spirit meant for surgical use. Their inebriated state would occasionally result in them being fully drunk during work hours, a situation that demanded immediate attention.

I was unsure how best to handle them without resorting to formal disciplinary action, which might jeopardise their livelihoods. One incident, however, pushed me close to the edge. Frustrated, I nearly struck one of them and delivered a stern threat, warning of interdiction if their behaviour continued. The gravity of my reaction seemed to resonate with them. They were apologetic, and while I suspected they may have continued their habit discreetly, I never caught them in the act again.

Interestingly, when sober, these individuals were diligent workers and kind-hearted people, which made the situation more complex as to why they were doing this act. This experience taught me a critical lesson in managing difficult personalities–to balance firmness with understanding and to lead with empathy while maintaining professional standards.

Lasting friendships

The nearest district hospital to Badalkumbura was in Passara, where Dr. Ajith Mendis served as the district medical officer (DMO). We quickly developed a strong friendship, often meeting over a few drinks and having deep conversations that solidified our bond. Passara became a regular meeting spot, conveniently located on my route to Badulla, and through Dr. Mendis , I was introduced to an incredible circle of friends who enriched my time in the region.

Dr. Mendis's network included tea planters and other professionals from the surrounding estates, whose colonial-era bungalows became venues for weekly gatherings. These evenings were filled with camaraderie, laughter, and music, creating moments of joy that have left an indelible mark on my memory.

Among the many wonderful people I met through Dr. Mendis, one stood out as an exceptional and rare gem: Lalith Panditharatna, a private rubber planter near Badalkumbura. Lalith was more than a friend; he was a loyal companion, the kind one is lucky to find even once in a lifetime. He had an unmatched generosity of spirit and was always there when I needed support.

At one point, when I was struggling to find a suitable chef (cook) for my residence, Lalith stepped in and managed to find one of his own staff members for me. Not only that, but he also took care of the chef's expenses for an extended period, an act of kindness that I will never forget. Sadly, Lalith's life was cut tragically short when he passed away while still young, leaving a void that was deeply felt by everyone who knew him.

At the time of his passing, I was in Australia and unable to attend his funeral, a regret that has stayed with me to today. Lalith was a selfless individual who cared deeply for his friends, though I often felt he did not prioritise his own well-being. His memory remains alive in my heart, as he attended our wedding, and his daughter had the honour of being our flower girl, a role that added a touch of his enduring presence to our special day.

Some of the friendships I formed through Dr. Mendis, such as with Salinda Madugalla, another tea planter have stood the test of time, and we still communicate regularly, even after more than forty years. Others, like OIC Gamunu Baddewela, have sadly passed away, yet their memories remain cherished. Through Ajith I also met key figures in the region, including the assistant government agent (AGA), the police inspector, the inspector of telecommunications, and many other planters and friends. This growing circle of friends and acquaintances made navigating the challenges of rural healthcare far easier.

Dr. Mendis himself went on to achieve remarkable heights in his career, eventually becoming the regional director of health services (RDHS) in Badulla and, later, the director general of health services (DGHS) in Sri Lanka. Despite his busy and illustrious career, we remained close friends, sharing bond that endured through the years to this date.

The friendships and connections I formed during this period in my medical journey were as significant as the professional milestones I achieved. Whether it was the warmth of Lalith's generosity, the laughter shared with Ajith and his network of friends, or the enduring ties that continue to this day among colleagues, these relationships enriched my life immeasurably.

They reminded me that in the simplest of settings, amidst the challenges of rural life, one can find the greatest gifts of all: genuine human connection and unwavering support. These friendships taught me the value of loyalty, kindness, and shared experiences, leaving memories that I carry with me to this day.

The rural life

During my time in Badalkumbura, someone, either a staff member, a patient, or even a member of the Gunasekera family, suggested I try my hand at sugarcane cultivation. The idea intrigued me, as it seemed like a novel way to engage with the rural community while diversifying my experiences. So, I decided to try it, leasing a small plot in a remote village about 2 to 3 miles from Badalkumbura.

The venture lasted about a year or two before I eventually gave it up, due to lack of time but it was an interesting chapter, nonetheless. The caretakers of the sugarcane estate were warm and hospitable, turning my occasional visits into moments of simple joy. They would greet me with a glass or two of freshly tapped toddy, a local palm wine, and serve cassava, prepared fresh and steaming. These moments, seated under the shade of trees while enjoying the company of the caretakers and the serenity of the estate, offered a peaceful escape from my busy schedule at the hospital.

Life in rural Sri Lanka came with its own unique rewards, particularly when it came to the abundance of wild game. Patients and locals often brought gifts of freshly hunted wild boar meat and other exotic meats as tokens of appreciation for the care they received at the hospital. These gestures were humbling and reflected the deep gratitude and respect the community had for its doctor. The food culture of the area was deeply tied to the land, so the taste of these rural delicacies was unlike anything I had experienced before. It was another way of connecting with the local community and gaining a deeper appreciation for their way of life.

What struck me most about Badalkumbura was the unwavering kindness of its people. In their eyes, a doctor was more than just a professional. At times, they treated me as if I were a guardian or even a deity. Their reverence was often overwhelming, but it was also deeply touching. This was not an unusual characteristic of many rural Sri Lankans.

Within the hospital, I had the privilege of working with a few loyal staff members who would go above and beyond their duties to ensure my comfort and well-being, becoming the backbone of my experience in Badalkumbura. They not only made my professional life easier but also took care of me on a personal level, ensuring I never feel alone or unsupported.

My time in Badalkumbura was filled with diverse and enriching experiences, from trying my hand at sugarcane farming to sharing meals with the locals and experiencing their unmatched hospitality. While the sugarcane cultivation venture may not have been a long-term success, the memories of toddy, cassava, and laughter with the caretakers are moments I treasure.

These experiences, coupled with the unwavering kindness of the community and the loyalty of my staff, remain some of the most cherished memories of my life at that time. They reminded me of the power of human connection, the richness of rural life, and the profound impact of simple acts of kindness.

A punctured hope

Unfortunately, one of the most tragic events of my career occurred during my time in Badalkumbura, an experience that still haunts me to this day. It involved a United Nations Medical Officer from Burma who was working alongside me at the time. He lived in a government bungalow next to mine with his young family, and his wife was pregnant with their second child.

The couple had decided to manage her delivery at home, with her husband taking responsibility for the procedure. It was a decision rooted in confidence in his own skills but one that would tragically demonstrate the risks of treating one's own family, particularly in high-stakes situations.

One afternoon, he rushed to my residence in visible distress, emotions written all over his face as he pleaded with me to come to his bungalow immediately. When we arrived, I was confronted with a harrowing sight- his wife lying on the bed, her clothes soaked in blood.

Trying to steady himself, the officer explained what had happened. The delivery of the baby had been uneventful, but complications arose with the placenta shortly after. It had not expelled after the delivery, and to remove it manually, he had applied traction to the umbilical cord. Unfortunately, his efforts failed, and worse, the cord broke, leaving the placenta intact inside the uterus.

His wife began to haemorrhage, and it was clear that she was in grave danger. I immediately recognised the signs of a potential placenta accreta, a rare but severe condition where the placenta adheres to the uterine muscle, making expulsion difficult or impossible without surgical intervention. So, we sprang into action. Knowing that every second counted, we arranged for the hospital's ambulance and started her on an intravenous drip to stabilise her condition as much as possible. I contacted the Badulla General Hospital, about forty kilometres away, and explained the critical nature of the situation. They assured me that they would prepare for an emergency blood transfusion and the need for a hysterectomy to stop the bleeding. I informed my friend Dr. Ajith about the situation, who had also contacted the Badulla General Hospital and arranged everything in preparation for the patient's arrival.

The journey to Badulla began with the medical officer and me accompanying his wife in the ambulance. Every kilometre felt like an eternity as we raced against time, knowing the consequences of any delay. Just as we passed Passara, about six kilometres from Badulla, the unthinkable happened: The ambulance had a tyre puncture. To make matters worse, the spare tyre was not in a usable condition. Panic set in as we tried to think of a solution, and desperately, we contacted Badulla General Hospital and requested another ambulance.

The delay felt unbearable. When the second ambulance finally arrived, we transferred her as quickly as possible, but precious time had already been lost. The sense of helplessness was overwhelming. When we finally reached Badulla General Hospital, the team was ready and immediately began administering blood transfusions. Despite their best efforts, the extensive haemorrhage had already taken its toll. Within hours, his wife succumbed to her condition.

Her death was devastating for her husband, who had to grapple with both grief and guilt, and for me, as I watched life slip away despite every effort to save her. This incident remains one of the most heart-wrenching experiences of my medical career, underscoring the fragility of life and the unpredictability of medical complications, even in controlled situations.

For me, the greatest takeaway was a reaffirmation of the principle: never treat your own family members. Emotional involvement clouds judgment and can lead to decisions that might not be in the patient's best interest. For her husband, it was a painful lesson in the limitations of one's skills when emotions are involved. For me, it was a sombre reminder of the profound responsibility we bear as healthcare professionals and the importance of always striving to minimise preventable tragedies.

This incident left an indelible mark on me, shaping the way I approached patient care in the years that followed. It was a heartbreaking chapter in my time at Badalkumbura, but one that reinforced the need for humility, vigilance, and constant improvement in the practice of medicine.

A chance meeting that changed my life

During this vibrant period of my life, filled with professional success and a rich social circle, fate had a surprise in store for me. One day, I decided to travel to Colombo to attend to some personal matters. Wanting company and someone to share the drive, I asked my good friend Sumith to join me. He happily agreed, and on the way, he suggested we stop in Panadura and stay overnight at the home of his uncle's wife (who happened to be my now-wife's sister), where we could rest before continuing to Colombo the next day.

The idea sounded appealing, and I was happy with the arrangement. Little did I know that this ordinary detour would lead to one of the most pivotal moments of my life. At the house in Panadura, I was warmly welcomed by the family. During our short stay, my attention was drawn to a beautiful girl in her early twenties who captured my heart instantly. She had long, flowing hair that reached down to her knees and a slender, graceful build. There was something about her presence that stirred something deep within me–a feeling I had not experienced before.

As luck would have it, she had a mild cough at the time, which gave me the perfect excuse to interact with her. Taking my professional role as a doctor seriously, I wrote her a prescription, hoping it might give me another opportunity to see her or speak to her again. The family treated us with great warmth, and her mother, a pleasant and elegant woman, left a strong impression on me as well. The next morning, Sumith and I continued our journey to Colombo, but my thoughts kept drifting back to her.

In the days that followed, I could not get her out of my mind. Finally, I found an excuse to call her, using her cough as the reason. When she answered the phone, I nervously asked about her health. Though I cannot recall the exact words we exchanged, I remember the way the conversation flowed. One topic led to another, and before I knew it, we had developed a connection.

Our relationship grew gradually; over the next few months, we exchanged letters and had occasional phone calls, each conversation bringing us closer together. With time, the frequency of our calls increased, as did my feelings for her.

A few months later, her family visited Badalkumbura, staying with the Gunasekera family, who had been like a second family to me. I took the opportunity to organise a trip to Pasikuda, a stunning coastal destination, hoping to spend more time with her there.

During the trip, amidst the beautiful beaches and serene surroundings, I had the chance to talk to Luckmalie more deeply and get to know her better. These moments solidified my feelings for her, and I knew in my heart that I wanted to spend my life with her. It took only seven months from the day I met her to decide I wanted to propose. When I expressed my feelings to her, she suggested I speak directly to her parents.

Though nervous, I gathered the courage to call her at home to talk with her parents. During a conversation with her mother, I openly shared that we were in love and that I wished to marry their daughter. The initial response was not what I had hoped for, as her mother expressed concern that our horoscopes did not match, a traditional barrier in Sri Lankan culture. While respectful of their beliefs, I could not accept that a horoscope could dictate the course of our lives.

Her mother, a smart and articulate woman, engaged in a thoughtful conversation with me, so I asked her how something as abstract as astrology could define love, compatibility, and the future of two individuals. Though it took some time, I eventually won her over with patience, sincerity, and logic. After a fair amount of deliberation, her parents gave us their blessing, and our relationship was formalised. It was a moment of immense joy for both of us, marking the beginning of a new chapter.

On May 11, 1984, we were married, surrounded by family and friends, beginning a journey that continues to bring love, partnership, and meaning to my life even today. Our wedding was a modest yet joyful affair, held at one of my wife's uncles' homes in Nugegoda. While it was not an extravagant ceremony, it was steeped in traditional practices that honoured both our families' cultures and values. Surrounded by close family members and friends I had grown close to over the past four years, the event was intimate and filled with heartfelt moments.

Among those who stood by us on this special day was Gamini Athukorala, who signed as my witness, and Rupa Karunathilake, who signed as a witness on behalf of my wife. They were two government ministers known to us in person. The reception was lively, featuring live music, drinks, and a delicious lunch, creating a warm and celebratory atmosphere.

For our honeymoon, we planned a unique getaway, blending relaxation with exploration. We spent our first night at a cozy hotel in Wadduwa before venturing to various tea estate bungalows where my friends were estate superintendents. These bungalows, nestled in the breathtaking landscapes of the hill country, offered a perfect escape for the two of us.

After our wedding, my wife joined me in Badalkumbura, where we spent a few weeks before making the move to Keppetipola/Welimada. This transitional period was filled with anticipation and excitement as we prepared to embark on this new chapter together.

One of the memorable gestures that added to the experience was a gift from my wife's uncle–a bottle of Hennessy VSOP, which became a delightful companion during our honeymoon. The combination of scenic views, cool climates, and the warmth of hospitality from friends made these early days of married life truly unforgettable.

Looking back, I often marvel at the chain of events that led to meeting my wife. From an unexpected stop in Panadura to a mild cough that gave me an excuse to connect with her, it all feels like fate played a significant role. What began as a chance encounter blossomed into a lifelong bond, proving that the most profound connections often arise in the most unexpected ways. This period not only brought love into my life but also reinforced the value of courage, sincerity, and persistence in pursuing what truly matters.

A fresh start in the hill country

Before our wedding, I had already decided to seek a transfer closer to Nuwara Eliya, a region I had always been drawn to for its cold, fresh climate, and picturesque landscapes. This desire to start our married life in a serene environment, away from the demanding workload of Badalkumbura, aligned with my eligibility for a transfer after four years of service at the hospital.

I set my sights on a health centre in Keppetipola, which was about a thirty-minute drive from Nuwara Eliya and fifteen kilometres away. The idea of working in a place with a lighter workload appealed to me, as it would give me more time to focus on my newly wedded life and enjoy the peace and charm of the hill country.

Arranging the transfer was made smoother with the help of some influential friends and well-wishers. The local Member of Parliament and government minister for the Welimada electorate, the late Percy Samaraweera, played a key role in expediting the process.

This connection was facilitated by the late Baddewela, a police inspector I had befriended during my time in Passara. His introduction to Percy Samaraweera was instrumental in ensuring the transfer moved forward without delays. The support I received from these individuals underscored the importance of the friendships and connections I had nurtured over the years.

Settling into the colder climate and serene beauty of the hill country felt like a natural continuation of the life I had envisioned for my wife and I. It offered not just a fresh environment but also the promise of shared experiences, personal growth, and building a life together.

Looking back, the period surrounding our wedding and honeymoon was a time of profound joy and transformation. It was not just about getting married: it was about transitioning into a new phase of life, supported by love, friendships, and the promise of new beginnings.

The move to Keppetipola marked the start of a chapter that combined professional fulfilment with personal happiness, setting the stage for the journey that lay ahead. Compared to my earlier life in Badalkumbura, the pace in the hill country was quieter and more focused, but it was also filled with new experiences, responsibilities, and personal growth.

Adjusting to a new life

The number of parties and social gatherings diminished significantly after the move to the hill country. While I continued to maintain friendships with my old circle, the frequency of our meetings naturally decreased. However, our association with prominent figures such as Samaraweera, the local Member of Parliament, and other influential acquaintances helped us build a new social network in Keppetipola. We also grew close to the Member of Parliament for Uva Paranagama, whose residence was conveniently located near the health centre. Their family often sought my medical advice, which fostered a bond between us, while my wife struck up a friendship with Mrs. Karunarathna, who would later rise to prominence as a deputy minister in the UNP government.

Workwise, Keppetipola was much quieter than Badalkumbura. The pace of the health centre was manageable, leaving me more time to focus on building a private practice, much like the one I had developed in Badalkumbura.

My private practice was based at our official residence, and my wife became an integral part of it. In addition to managing household responsibilities, she actively assisted me by dispensing medications and handling patient charges. I taught her how to read prescriptions, to which she learned quickly, becoming a capable and reliable partner in my practice. This work was different to what she had done before the marriage, which was a quantity surveyor working for a private firm, but she happily resigned from her job on my request before the marriage.

About four months after we were married, my wife became pregnant with our eldest daughter, Poornima. The pregnancy was challenging, as my wife experienced severe nausea and vomiting (Hyperemesis Gravidarum) throughout the term, right up until the day of delivery. Despite the difficulties, we were thrilled to welcome our daughter into the world.

For her confinement, we chose Badulla General Hospital, where I had professional ties with the obstetrician. The delivery was uneventful, and Poornima arrived healthy and strong. Watching my wife transition into motherhood while continuing to assist me in my practice was inspiring, as her resilience and dedication were remarkable.

Just months after Poornima's birth, my wife became pregnant again with our second child, Chaturanga. As with her first pregnancy, she suffered from Hyperemesis Gravidarum, making the journey equally demanding with being a mom of a baby and working. This time, however, there were additional complications. We opted again for Badulla General Hospital for delivery, but the circumstances were less favourable. Unlike during the first pregnancy, we could not secure a private room, so she had to stay in a public ward. The conditions were less than ideal: the wards were overcrowded, and the hygiene, especially in the toilets, left much to be desired.

My wife was deeply upset about being left in such a setting, and it took her some time to forgive me for what she saw as a lapse in care due to poor hygiene and overcrowding. I felt her frustration acutely but believed it was the best decision for her safety, given the circumstances. During the later stages of her pregnancy, the obstetrician expressed concern about the baby's maturity, unsure if it was full-term based on her last menstrual period. He advised that we travel to Kandy General Hospital to have an X-ray reviewed by a specialist radiologist, adding further stress to the situation.

The results of the X-ray revealed that the baby was full-term and ready for delivery. However, since my wife did not go into natural labour, the obstetrician decided to induce labour using a Syntocinon infusion. Thankfully, my wife's uterus responded well to the induction, and she delivered our son, Chaturanga, without any major complications. Despite the initial challenges and the emotional toll of the experience, the safe delivery of our son brought immense joy to our growing family.

The transition to life in Keppetipola was not without its challenges, but it also brought profound happiness. It was here that our family began to grow, both in size and in strength. My wife's unwavering support in both my professional and personal life was instrumental in making this period of my life fulfilling.

Through the trials of pregnancy and parenthood, the demands of private practice, and the connections we built in the community, Keppetipola became a place of new beginnings and lasting memories.

Shortly after settling into Keppetipola, my wife's youngest brother Neminda , who was about 12 years old at the time, 13 years younger than my wife, expressed a strong desire to visit her. His attachment to his sister was evident as he insisted on coming to spend time with us. Recognising how much he missed her, his parents arranged for him to join St. Thomas' College in Guruthalawa, a well-reputed school near to Keppetipola; this allowed him to travel between the school and our home with relative ease, taking just two buses. Having him with us brought a fresh dynamic to our household, and his youthful energy and humour became a delightful addition to our lives.

One particularly amusing incident still stands out in my memory. During one of her visits to Keppetipola, my mother-in-law stayed with us. Her youngest son, despite being twelve years old, was still deeply attached to her, often choosing to sleep beside her.

One afternoon, after returning from school, we encouraged him to sit down and study. However, he resisted the idea, as most young boys do, preferring anything over opening his books. My mother-in-law, ever-nurturing, decided to coax him into studying by taking him to bed and asking him to read while lying down. Predictably, he dozed off instead of studying.

Hearing the commotion of my mother-in-law trying to wake him up, I peeked into the room to see what was happening. The scene was both hilarious and revealing of his cleverness. As I asked what was going on, he opened his eyes and, without missing a beat, said, "Aiya (Brother), I was just contemplating my studies with my eyes closed. Amma (Mother) thought I was sleeping!" It was a classic moment of quick wit and charm that highlighted his ability to navigate situations with humour and intelligence.

During his time with us, he grew close to our children, forming a special bond with them. His playful nature and willingness to engage made him a helpful and caring presence in their lives. Whether it was playing games with them or simply keeping them entertained, he became an integral part of the household. Despite his mischievous streak, his presence brought joy and laughter, making our home in Keppetipola even more lively and memorable.

Keppetipola offered no shortage of humorous and unforgettable incidents that became cherished family stories for us. One such episode involved a young boy who came to the health centre with a lacerated wound that needed suturing. As I began stitching, the boy, in pain or simply overwhelmed by the situation, started calling me "Puke Mahattaya," which translates to "Master of the Anal." It was a completely random and nonsensical nickname, but he chanted it with such enthusiasm and repetition that I could not help but chuckle, even as I focused on finishing the suturing. My wife, who was present, found the whole situation hilarious. She laughed uncontrollably and continued to remind me of the incident for years, teasing me by repeating the boy's chant whenever the mood struck.

Amid these light-hearted moments, life in Keppetipola also brought milestones worth celebrating. Shortly after I got married, I fulfilled a long-standing dream of owning a brand-new car. Using the money I had saved, and a generous gift from my wife's wealthy uncle, I ordered a Honda Civic directly from Japan. The car, a stunning red model, arrived soon after we had settled into Keppetipola. The vibrant red vehicle quickly became a symbol of my presence in the area. Patients and locals alike began associating me with the car, referring to me as the doctor with the red Honda Civic. It brought a sense of distinction, helping me establish myself within the community and elevating my status among local leaders.

While material milestones like the new car were exciting, what truly made my time in Keppetipola special was the kindness and respect of the local community. People in the area were polite and pleasant, showing deep gratitude for the care they received. Their genuine warmth made my work more fulfilling and left a lasting impression on my heart. From the amusing chants of a playful, young boy to the pride of owning my first new car, my time in Keppetipola was filled with unique and meaningful moments. These experiences, whether light-hearted or life-changing, reflect the joy of connecting with people and the richness of rural life, remaining some of the most treasured memories of my journey.

Scary hospital experience

One ordinary day at the health centre turned into one of the most nerve-wracking moments of my career. After completing my morning consultations in the outpatient department (OPD), I returned to my residence, conveniently located next door, for a brief tea break. It was around 10:30 a.m., and I noticed that a parent with a child had arrived to my residence, seeking my attention for a private consultation. Since they had been waiting for some time, I decided to see the child right away.

As I was attending to them, one of my staff members hurriedly approached me, looking visibly flustered. They informed me that someone from the head office had arrived unexpectedly and was asking for me at the health centre.

Rushing back to the health centre, I was shocked to find none other than the late Secretary of the Ministry of Health, Dr. Malinga Fernando, waiting for me. Renowned for his strict demeanour and no-nonsense approach, he was someone whose presence often sent shivers down the spines of health workers across the department. As soon as I arrived, he wasted no time in questioning my absence during working hours, his tone firm and direct. "Why were you not at the health centre?" he demanded.

Caught off guard, I knew that admitting I had been seeing a private patient at my residence was not an option. Thinking quickly, I replied, "I had to go to the toilet, so I went to my residence." His reply was dripping with sarcasm. "Ah yes, it seems whenever we visit, you people feel the need to go to the toilet!" His expression made it clear he was not convinced by my response, but he did not press further at that moment.

Dr. Fernando stayed at the health centre for only a brief time, but he nevertheless conducted a thorough inspection, checking several registers and spending some time in the pharmacy/dispensary, reviewing the procedures and inventory. Although his visit did not last long, his reputation and stern approach left everyone in the health centre on edge.

As he departed, I could not shake the anxiety about what might follow. Dr. Fernando was known for taking swift action when he found irregularities, and I braced myself for the worst. A few weeks later, a letter from the Health Department arrived bearing Dr. Fernando's signature. My heart raced as I opened it, fearing the repercussions of his visit. The letter was a formal request for an explanation as to why I had been absent from the health centre during official working hours.

Nervously, I drafted my response, confirming the same explanation I had given him verbally during his visit: That I had been at my residence to use the toilet. It was not the most convincing excuse, but it was the only one I could provide without further incriminating myself.

To my relief, there was no further action. The matter was dropped, likely because Dr. Fernando had more pressing issues to address elsewhere. I will never know whether he believed my explanation or simply decided it was not worth pursuing.

This incident served as a powerful reminder of the importance of being vigilant and always maintaining professionalism. While I was fortunate to avoid profound consequences, the experience left a lasting impression on me. It underscored the need to balance private practice with official duties carefully and to always be prepared for the unexpected, especially when dealing with high-ranking officials. Despite the stress, I can now look back on this episode with a mix of amusement and relief, grateful that it remained a cautionary tale rather than a career-altering event.

Local connections

During my time in Keppetipola, I had the opportunity to visit several mobile health centres established for the benefit of local communities. These trips were both rewarding and enjoyable, as they allowed me to connect with the people in remote villages who often lacked access to basic healthcare.

The villagers, grateful for the services, were incredibly hospitable to me, and often brought me fresh vegetables from their gardens or produce from their farms as tokens of appreciation. These gestures reflected the warmth and generosity of the rural community, making these visits memorable highlights of my time there.

Keppetipola was not just a workplace; it became a place where I forged strong relationships with a wide array of people, from local politicians and community leaders to temple monks and government servants. By this point in my career, I had come to understand the power of influence and how important it was to maintain good relationships with key individuals in the community.

One of my most trusted allies was the Officer in Charge of the Welimada Police Station, the late Gamunu Baddewela. We had first met during my time in Badalkumbura, introduced by my good friend Dr. Mendis, and his presence in Keppetipola gave me a sense of confidence and security. Tragically, not long after my arrival in Keppetipola, he passed away due to an illness. His sudden death came as a great shock to me and to everyone who knew him.

Located directly across from the health centre was the bus depot of the Ceylon Transport Board (CTB), or as it is now known, the Sri Lanka Transport Board (SLTB). Many CTB employees would visit me, not only for medical consultations but also for medical certificates (MCs). While some of these requests were genuine, others were more opportunistic.

A few employees would ask for extra days off to extend their time away from work. Some even asked if I could retroactively cover the days they had not worked, claiming to have been unwell. While I was hesitant to indulge such requests, I occasionally obliged, wanting to maintain goodwill.

However, this practice nearly landed me in serious trouble. The depot manager, noticing a pattern of absenteeism among employees, lodged a formal complaint with the health department, accusing me of issuing unwarranted medical certificates. This triggered a visit from the department's flying squad, tasked with auditing my patient records and reviewing the counterfoils of all the medical certificates I had issued.

The audit was a nerve-wracking experience. Thankfully, most of my records were in good order, and most of the certificates were found to be valid and adequately documented. However, there were a few cases where I could not provide substantial evidence to justify the issuance of medical certificates; for those instances, I had to prepare detailed explanations to defend my actions. It was a tense period, as the potential repercussions could have been severe. Fortunately, my explanations were accepted, and no further action was taken against me.

This episode taught me some critical lessons about balancing empathy and professionalism. While I valued maintaining positive relationships with the community, I realised the importance of adhering strictly to protocol and not letting goodwill compromise ethical standards.

Keppetipola continued to be a place of both growth and challenges, shaping my approach to community healthcare and professional integrity. The warmth of the villagers, the friendships I built, and even the occasional hurdles I faced all contributed to my understanding of leadership, responsibility, and the delicate balance required to serve a community effectively.

CHAPTER 4

The Janatha Vimukthi Peramuna Insurrection of 1989 and Leaving My Motherland

By the late 1980s, Sri Lanka was mired in political and social unrest. The JVP had grown increasingly disillusioned with the ruling government's policies, particularly its perceived capitulation to foreign powers through the Indo-Lanka Accord in 1987, which brought Indian forces to the island as peacekeepers. This, coupled with rising unemployment, economic hardship, and political discontent, fuelled a rebellious attitude among the people. The movement, once an idealistic revolutionary front, transformed into a brutal and violent insurgency, engaging in acts of sabotage, assassinations, and intimidation to challenge state authority.

This culminated in 1989, in a dark and tumultuous chapter in Sri Lanka's history, as the country was gripped by the second insurrection of the Janatha Vimukthi Peramuna (JVP). What had begun as a left-wing nationalist movement in the 1970s transformed into a violent rebellion fuelled by deep socio-economic grievances and political unrest.

At the core of the uprising was the disillusionment of Sri Lanka's youth with a political system they perceived as corrupt and unresponsive to their needs. The rebellion was further intensified by the presence of the Indian Peace Keeping Force (IPKF), which had been deployed under a contentious Indo-Sri Lankan agreement. The JVP, fiercely opposed to the

IPKF's presence, rallied nationalist sentiments to garner support, but their methods plunged the country into chaos.

The rebellion quickly escalated into a period of widespread terror and violence. Government officials, military personnel, and civilians were targeted, as the JVP used tactics that included assassinations, arson, and economic sabotage. The insurgents imposed crippling strikes, disrupted daily life, and silenced dissent with fear and intimidation.

The government, in turn, responded with a heavy hand, employing counter-insurgency measures that often blurred the lines between law enforcement and human rights violations. Thousands of people, many of them innocent, disappeared or were killed during this period. The entire country was engulfed in a climate of mistrust and paranoia, and no one was immune to the violence.

As a medical professional in the Uva region, I had a front-row seat to the human cost of the insurrection. Though relatively remote, even rural areas like Keppetipola were not spared from the JVP's influence and the government's countermeasures. The atmosphere was thick with fear, and daily life was a delicate balance between fulfilling my professional duties and ensuring my personal safety and that of my family.

The insurrection posed profound moral and ethical dilemmas for individuals caught in its wake. The insurgents demanded loyalty, often threatening violence against those who did not comply with their demands. On the other hand, the government was equally suspicious of anyone who might be aiding or sympathising with the JVP, leading to arbitrary arrests and detentions.

In this fraught environment, neutrality became a survival strategy. As a doctor, I focused on my role as a healthcare professional, refusing to take sides while providing care to those in need. However, maintaining this balance was not easy, as both insurgents and government forces were wary of perceived allegiances.

This period profoundly impacted my outlook on life, leadership, and resilience, reinforcing the importance of remaining steadfast in one's principles, even in the face of adversity. The experience taught me how to navigate uncertainty and fear, relying on integrity and compassion as guiding principles.

It also deepened my understanding of the socio-political complexities of Sri Lanka and the vulnerabilities of its people. I emerged from the insurrection with a stronger sense of purpose and a renewed commitment to making a difference in people's lives, knowing how fragile peace and stability could be.

Local terror

While the JVP insurrection left scars that are still visible today, it also highlighted the resilience of the Sri Lankan people. The rebellion was crushed, but at a devastating cost–tens of thousands of lives lost and a legacy of fear that would take years to overcome.

For me, this chapter served as a defining moment, shaping not only my career but also my perspective on service, community, and humanity. It was a time that tested our collective resolve and left an indelible mark on all who lived through it.

The rural areas, such as Welimada and Badulla, were not immune to the violence and fear that enveloped the country. Being less urbanised, these regions were marked by a closer-knit community fabric, which made the presence of insurgents and government forces more terrifying for civilians. The hilly terrains and remote villages in these regions provided strategic cover for JVP militants who sought refuge while launching operations against government forces.

Civilians were caught in a brutal crossfire between the JVP and the military. Curfews became a constant reality in these regions, often imposed by both the government and the JVP in their efforts to control movement. These curfews not only crippled daily life but also left residents in a perpetual state of fear, as even venturing out for essential supplies could lead to deadly encounters.

The JVP was notorious for using government employees, including schoolteachers and clerks, as human shields or forcing them to participate in rallies and demonstrations. The use of public servants as shields in these regions, where government influence was more limited, was a strategy to deter government retaliation.

Public servants also were coerced into attending rallies or paying "donations" to the movement under threat of death. If they failed to comply, they were labelled as traitors or government informants, often leading to their brutal assassinations by the JVP.

The period was marked by terror for ordinary people as the JVP imposed its own laws in areas under its control, brutally punishing anyone they suspected of being sympathetic to the government or failing to comply with their demands. Nighttime brought a particularly deep sense of dread, as unknown individuals could knock on doors, whisking away civilians who were never seen again. Forced disappearances became common, with young men and civilians often taken from their homes by either the JVP or government forces, or some unknown groups never to return. Many of them were executed and their bodies were displayed to be seen by people.

The government, in response to the insurgency, also resorted to heavy-handed tactics, as mentioned above. Paramilitary groups and military units carried out counter-insurgency operations that led to extrajudicial killings and disappearances. Civilians often became collateral damage in the efforts to root out insurgents in the villages. The widespread distrust between civilians, the government, and the JVP led to an atmosphere of paranoia and suspicion. People were afraid to speak freely or trust their neighbours, as even a whispered conversation could result in someone being accused of supporting one side or the other, often with deadly consequences.

In the Welimada and Badulla regions, roads were often deserted after dark due to the fear of abductions and killings. Both the JVP and government forces engaged in targeted killings, and civilians had to navigate a delicate line to avoid being labelled as sympathisers of either faction. For many families, the terror of hearing footsteps outside their doors late at night was a recurring nightmare. No one was certain who would be next.

Public spaces became battlegrounds for demonstrations organised by the JVP, which were often orchestrated in defiance of government-imposed curfews. These rallies were not just expressions of defiance but also of desperation, as the JVP sought to mobilise the rural populace to revolt against the state. Civilians were frequently forced to participate in these rallies, with the threat of violence looming large.

In these regions, the army often responded to such rallies with force, leading to violent clashes, mass arrests, and sometimes outright massacres. The aftermath of such confrontations saw a further entrenchment of fear as people grew increasingly distrustful of both the insurgents and the state. The villagers of Welimada and Badulla, already grappling with economic hardship due to the conflict, faced the additional burden of navigating the volatile political landscape.

The insurgency claimed thousands of lives, many of them innocent civilians caught between the JVP's brutal methods and the government's equally ruthless crackdown. The Badulla and Welimada regions were no exception to this, with many residents witnessing friends, neighbours, and family members vanish overnight, leaving behind nothing but unanswered questions and unhealed wounds.

This time was the most horrific time in my life too. I tried to avoid the conflicts, avoid any known meetings or demonstrations, and leave Keppetipola and stay with one of our family friends in Nuwara Eliya. Fortunately, the JVP never forced me to attend a demonstration or meeting. I did not know who their ranks and members were and completely avoided any conversation that was political in nature.

One day, as I travelled along the main road from Welimada to Nuwara Eliya, I encountered a sight so horrifying that it remains etched in my memory to this day. Along the roadside, severed heads had been gruesomely mounted on the tips of sticks, lining the road like a grotesque display of terror.

I later learned that these were allegedly the heads of suspected JVP members, killed by government-sponsored groups or forces as part of the counter-insurgency efforts. The sight was both macabre and deeply unsettling, a stark reminder of the brutality that had engulfed the nation during this dark period.

For a moment, I considered taking a photograph of the gruesome display, but my wife, sensing the potential danger and unnecessary risk, strongly discouraged me. I am grateful for her caution because such an act could have been misinterpreted, leading to dire consequences. Still, the terrifying image lingered in my mind, a chilling symbol of the chaos that had overtaken our lives.

Life in Keppetipola during the JVP insurrection was fraught with fear and uncertainty, as they imposed strict curfews, dictating every aspect of daily life. One of their rules was that no one was allowed to keep lights on after a certain hour, forcing us to rely on the dim glow of a small oil lamp to get around.

This rule was not just an inconvenience; it created an atmosphere of intense fear. Our young children were often terrified, crying out of sheer panic as the darkness and silence closed in around us. As parents, my wife and I felt helpless, unsure of how to console them or even ensure their safety. The nights felt endless, each one stretching into an eternity of unease.

The threat of violence was omnipresent. On one occasion, the sound of a bomb blast nearby shook our residence so violently that we instinctively lifted our feet off the floor, feeling as if the explosion had occurred right next to us. Moments like these brought home the fragility of our situation, reminding us that we were living in the crosshairs of a conflict where safety was never guaranteed.

One night, one of our household aides, unaware of the risks, lit a lamp in the kitchen, violating the JVP-imposed blackout. Within minutes, stones were thrown at our roof, a chilling warning from those enforcing the curfew. Realising the danger, we immediately had the light extinguished and prayed that no further repercussions would follow.

Living under these conditions, we had to walk a tightrope, trying to navigate between obedience to the government and compliance with JVP demands. Any misstep could draw suspicion from one side or the other, putting our lives at risk. It was a precarious balancing act that required constant vigilance and often left us emotionally and physically drained.

These experiences were not just harrowing; they were transformative. They revealed the extremes of human behaviour, both the horrors of violence and the resilience required to endure it. The images, sounds, and emotions of that time remain vivid in my memory, serving as a haunting reminder of the fragility of peace and the preciousness of freedom. They are lessons that have shaped my outlook on life and my deep appreciation for stability and security.

One example of this lesson happened one evening, during a particularly tense year, when I was at my residence seeing private patients. My dispensary, located right next to our bedroom, was a place where I prepared and dispensed medications for those who came to consult me.

After completing a consultation, I stepped into the dispensary to prepare a prescription. As I reached out for one of the drug containers, I was struck with disbelief and terror. A large cobra, its hood raised, was perched next to the container I was about to touch.

The sight of the cobra sent a wave of panic through me. Instinctively, I shouted for my wife, urgently instructing her to secure our two young children, aged 3 and 4, who were fast asleep in the adjacent bedroom. My greatest fear was that the snake might slither into their room and hurt them.

Uncertain of what to do, I froze. Luckily, someone nearby heard the commotion and came to our aid. With remarkable bravery, they managed to capture the cobra and take it to a nearby turpentine plantation, where it was supposed to be released into the jungle. Later, we learned that the snake had been killed, a fact that left us deeply shaken.

This encounter lingered in my mind, not just for its immediate danger but also for the cultural and symbolic weight cobras carry. Stories abound of their association with prosperity, warnings, or destruction. Although I had never believed in such myths, the timing of the event was unsettling, as if foreshadowing the danger that lay ahead.

The night of terror

That night, as usual, we went to bed early, mindful of the curfew imposed either by the government or the JVP. The earlier cobra incident had left us anxious but unaware of what was to follow. Sometime past midnight, I woke to the sound of unusual human voices and the distinct noise of people running around our residence. My instincts told me something was terribly wrong. Moments later, there was a loud bang on our bedroom window, which faced the main gate.

We had all chosen to sleep in the same room that night, except for our domestic aide and my wife's younger brother, who were in separate rooms. I knew then that we were about to face something far more dangerous than a snake.

Steeling myself, I cautiously opened the window of my consultation room to see what was happening. Through the bars of the window, I saw a gun barrel pointed directly at me. A voice from the shadows ordered me to open the door. I realised there was no escape; any resistance would endanger not just my life but the lives of my wife and children. With no other option, I complied.

As I opened the door, a group of young men entered, carrying one of their wounded comrades who had gunshot wounds in his leg. The injuries were non-life-threatening, and from their explanation, the wounds had been caused by a misfire from one of their own weapons.

They demanded that I treat him immediately. With little choice, I began attending to the wounds, hoping to stabilise the injured man quickly and send them on their way. However, the gunshot wounds were complicated by deep-penetrating pellets, making it impossible for me to remove them on-site. I provided initial treatment and advised them to take the wounded man to Nuwara Eliya Hospital for surgery.

The group exchanged tense glances and stepped outside to discuss, leaving the injured man behind with me. A few minutes later, they returned, this time with an elderly woman, introduced as the wounded man's mother. They ordered me to personally transport the wounded man to Nuwara Eliya Hospital in my own private car. Along with the injured man and his mother, a third member of the group joined us, all sitting in the back seat of my car.

Before we left, they gave me a chilling reassurance: "Don't worry about your family; we will be here, watching over them." What was meant as a reassurance only deepened my fear. I realised their plan was calculated. The presence of the wounded man's mother was intended to minimise suspicion at military checkpoints, while I, as a doctor, had the curfew pass and professional credibility to transport a patient without raising alarms.

Reluctantly, I said goodbye to my wife, who stayed behind with our sleeping children, and began the nerve-wracking drive to Nuwara Eliya. On the way, we were stopped at a military checkpoint, and my heart pounded as armed officers approached the car. I introduced myself, explaining that I was transporting a patient to the hospital for treatment. To my immense relief, they allowed us to pass without further questions.

At Nuwara Eliya Hospital, I provided a brief to the admissions officer about the patient's condition and ensured the man was admitted for surgery. The two others, members of the group and the woman who had accompanied me stayed back at the hospital with their wounded comrade, allowing me to drive home alone. The journey back was filled with a mix of exhaustion, fear, and relief. When I arrived home, my wife was awake, waiting anxiously for my return. Seeing her and my children safe brought me an overwhelming sense of gratitude.

The aftermath of the terrifying night with the JVP militants left me shaken to my core. The very next day, I called my dear friend, Dr. Mendis, who was then the Regional Director of Health Services (RDHS) in Uva Province. I shared the details of the incident, including the forced treatment of the injured militant and the subsequent threats to my family. His advice was firm and unequivocal: "Leave Keppetipola immediately and report to the RDHS office."

Without hesitation, I followed his instructions. By morning, I had left Keppetipola and arrived at Badulla, seeking both safety and guidance. While I was in Badulla, my wife called, her voice trembling with fear. She told me that some JVP boys had returned, inquiring about my whereabouts and asking what arrangements had been made for their wounded comrade. Her fear was palpable, and my heart sank. I immediately spoke with Dr. Mendis about the situation. Understanding the gravity of the threat, he arranged for a vehicle to bring my wife and children to Badulla, ensuring their safety. That very day, we left Badulla for Panadura, seeking refuge with my wife's family.

Even with the safer location, peace eluded me. Sleepless nights became the norm, plagued by nightmares and the crushing realisation that I was now a target, not just for the JVP but for the government forces as well. It was a time when harbouring or treating a member of a proscribed terrorist organisation was considered a severe crime. By law, I should have reported the incident to the authorities. However, had I done so, I would have been targeted by the JVP for retaliation. There seemed to be no way out.

While in Panadura, I received a call from one of my staff members in Keppetipola. His tone was inquisitive, and he asked repeatedly about my whereabouts. I was deliberately evasive, suspecting that something was not right. My instincts were later proven correct; I found out that the police had arrested him and were using him to lure me out. Their intent was to arrest me for treating the JVP militant and failing to report the incident.

This revelation left me paralysed with fear; in those days, proper legal channels were not always followed. People suspected of aiding the JVP were arrested, detained, or, worse, they simply disappeared. Realising the gravity of my situation, I contacted the MP for Welimada, who was also a government minister. He knew me personally, as we had shared many conversations and social gatherings. I hoped he could intervene, and he advised me to meet the assistant superintendent of police (ASP) in Bandarawela and make a formal statement.

When I met the ASP, a Tamil gentleman, known for his fairness and professionalism, listened to my account with understanding but informed me, "Under the law, I have no choice but to arrest you and remand you." His words struck like a hammer. I pleaded for a few moments to speak with my wife, and he graciously agreed. In desperation, my wife contacted the MP for Uva Paranagama, Mrs Karunaratne, a deputy minister and a close family friend. This remarkable woman immediately called the ASP while I was still in his office. With conviction, she assured him of my innocence and personally vouched for me. The woman requested that I be released after providing a statement, and, to my immense relief, the ASP honoured her request.

However, the Officer-in-Charge (OIC) of the Welimada Police was far less forgiving. Angered that I had bypassed him and gone directly to the

ASP, he harboured resentment. I was warned by friends that he might still pursue action against me.

The Regional Director of Health in Badulla, understanding my plight, arranged for me to work temporarily at the Badulla General Hospital. However, the situation remained precarious. The ASP in charge of the anti-terrorist unit in Badulla was notorious for his ruthless tactics, and it was widely believed that he was responsible for the disappearances of many individuals suspected of JVP affiliations. Knowing that the OIC from Welimada and the Badulla ASP shared a close rapport, I realised I was still in grave danger. Dr. Mendis, the RDHS, ever the loyal friend, took me into his home and did everything he could to protect me.

Despite his efforts, I knew that remaining in Uva was no longer an option. Dr. Mendis helped secure a temporary placement at Colombo South General Hospital, where I could stay under the radar. After arriving in Colombo, I thought it marked the definitive end of my cherished dreams in the hill country. By then, I had purchased a beautiful piece of land in Bandarawela, with visions of a serene future. However, those dreams were dashed, and I sold the land. Moving to Panadura, my wife's hometown, my sole focus became leaving the country as quickly as possible.

I had lost all faith in the political system and leadership at the time; the notion of law and order seemed non-existent. The betrayal I felt extended beyond politics, seeping into the institutions meant to uphold justice and protect citizens.

When I returned to Keppetipola to collect my belongings, I was devastated to find that my residence had been robbed. Many of the items I had worked so hard for were gone. Feeling helpless but determined to seek justice, I went to the Welimada Police Station to file a report on the robbery.

Unfortunately, the officer-in-charge (OIC), who already harboured animosity toward me for bypassing him during the JVP incident, refused to entertain my complaint. Without a police report, I could not make an insurance claim for the stolen items; this deepened my disappointment and sense of betrayal.

Whispers reached me through trusted sources that the police themselves may have been involved in, or at least knowledgeable about, the robbery at the residence. If true, this would explain their refusal to assist. It was a cruel act of revenge for not reporting the wounded militant to them during the earlier incident.

However, I must emphasise that not all police officers or armed personnel during this tumultuous period were the same. Among the corruption and chaos, there were a few rare gems, individuals who embodied integrity and fairness. One such individual was the ASP in Bandarawela, a Tamil gentleman whose reputation for professionalism and fairness preceded him. Another was the police deputy inspector general (DIG) in Badulla, whose kindness and sense of duty shone through despite the overwhelming challenges of the time.

After repeatedly being resisted by the Welimada Police, I contacted the DIG Badulla and explained the situation. Without hesitation, he arranged for the necessary documents to be issued, enabling me to make an insurance claim for my losses. Their support was a ray of light in an otherwise bleak chapter of my life.

In these trying times, a few loyal friends stood by me as well, offering their unwavering support. Dr. Ajith Mendis, my trusted confidant mentioned earlier in the book, did everything he could to guide and protect me. Dr. Ratnayake, who was in Hali Ela at the time, also extended his hand when I needed it most. Their kindness reminded me that humanity and friendship could still prevail, even in the darkest times.

At Colombo South General Hospital, I reconnected with Professor Anton Jayasuriya, the internationally renowned authority for his work in acupuncture and complementary medicine, who had been instrumental in teaching acupuncture during my medical school days. Professor Jayasuriya was sympathetic to my plight and welcomed me into his team, as he understood my urgent need to leave Sri Lanka and offered to help. His frequent travels and international conferences presented a potential pathway for escape.

Professor Jayasuriya had an upcoming international conference in Norway, and we decided that I should apply for a visa to join his delegation. I was overjoyed when the visa was approved, believing this was my ticket to freedom. But my relief was short-lived. The very next day, I received a call from the Norwegian Embassy, asking me to return with my passport. To my dismay, they cancelled the visa, citing intelligence reports that certain individuals planned to use the conference as a cover to seek asylum. This setback felt like a devastating blow. My plans crumbled, and I was consumed by despair.

Leaving my motherland

During this time, my wife's elder brother, who was studying in Australia, became a beacon of hope. Professor Jayasuriya had strong ties with Australian medical organisations and regularly conducted courses and conferences there. Through these connections, he arranged for Dr. Andrew Ong, a general practitioner in Perth and a prominent figure in acupuncture, to send me an invitation letter to attend a conference in Australia. Armed with this letter, I applied for a visa to participate in the conference, and within days, the visa was approved. It felt like a lifeline in the darkest chapter of my life.

With a temporary visa and working rights, I bid farewell to Sri Lanka, the land of my birth, the land I had loved and served. But it was also a land that had failed to protect me when I needed it most.

As I boarded the plane, a mixture of relief and sorrow washed over me. I was grateful to those who had stood by me during this tumultuous time, but I also carried the weight of leaving behind a country that no longer felt like home. I felt apprehensive about leaving my wife and children in Sri Lanka, but I was determined to bring them to Australia as soon as practicable. I wanted to rebuild my life in Australia, carrying with me the lessons of resilience, the gratitude for those who had helped me, and the hope for a brighter future.

1. My parents' wedding photo

2. Our wedding in 1984

3. Our Wedding in 1984

4. At our homecomming with my Badalkumbura friends

5. With some staff members at Badalkumbura Hospital

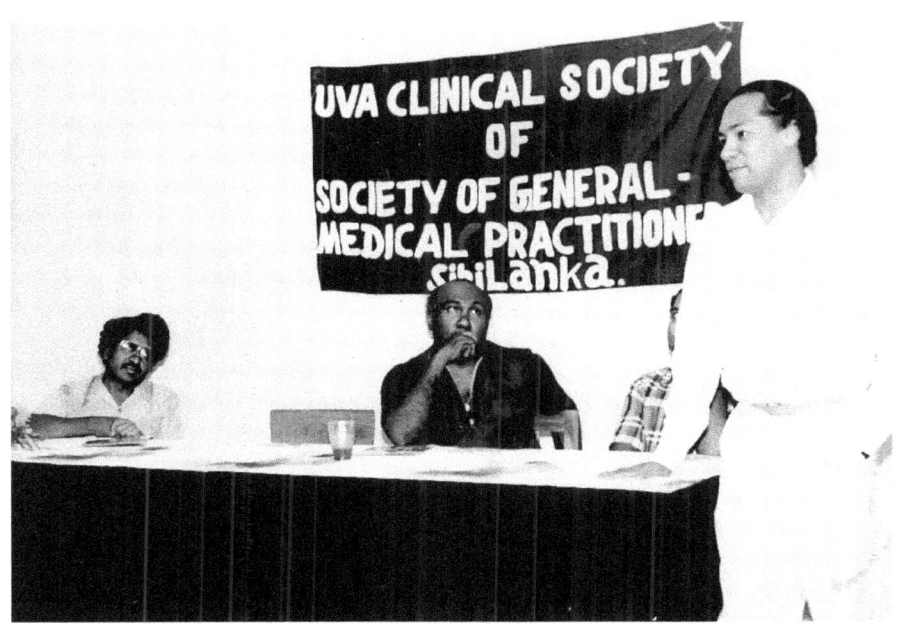

6. Taken in the 1980s when I was speaking at the Clinical Society I established in Sri Lanka. Seated are the Obstetrician, the General Surgeon, and an Anaesthetist from Badulla General Hospital

07. Poornima and Chaturanga while we were in Keppetipola

8. party time in Keppetipola

9. With Dr A Ong, taken in the 1990s

10. Demonstration in support of my acupuncture court case in front of the Perth Magistrates' Court.

11. After the victory in my acupuncture case, with some supporters outside the Perth Magistrates' Court

12. International Seminar On Acupuncure & Holisitic Medicine in KL, 1991

13. With the late Prof. Anton Jayasuriya

14. Investiture Ceremony in Perth

15. Taken after the investiture ceremony with some Sri Lankan friends outside St. Mary's Cathedral Perth

16. At the IUHS Graduation, the University Club Chicago, 2011

17. Family photo taken in 2014

18. Law graduation- UNE, NSW, 2018

19. With Dr Ajith Mendis, taken when I visited Sri Lanka in 2021

20. My two brothers, Ranjith (6th from the left) and Chaminda (far right), and my two sisters, Ramya (8th from the left) and Sandya (7th from the left), along with their families and Baby Uncle (in white)

21. AIHFE's final graduation before I sold it in 2024

CHAPTER 5

Opportunities and Legal Tribulations in Australia

On July 16, 1990, I embarked on a journey to redefine my life, leaving my wife and our two young children behind at her family home in Panadura, Sri Lanka. The emotions were mixed anticipation for the opportunities ahead and an ache for the family I was temporarily leaving behind. My wife's uncle, who was visiting Australia at the time to attend my brother-in-law's wedding, along with a friend of my brother-in-law, kindly came to Perth Airport to meet me. It was well past midnight by the time I arrived, and the wedding ceremony had just concluded. Exhausted yet exhilarated, I was taken to my brother-in-law's house, where I stayed temporarily with my wife's uncle.

The next morning, I wasted no time settling in and went to meet Dr. Ong, affectionately called "Andrew," at his surgery facility in Willetton. Andrew was not only expecting me but also extended a warm and heartfelt welcome, immediately making me feel at ease in a new land. He had an infectious energy and a cheerful disposition that were hard to miss. My role, as he explained, was to assist him in organising the World International Conference on complementary medicine and acupuncture. This would be a pivotal event, held over three days in November 1990, with its main sessions at the Hilton Hotel in Perth and clinical workshops scheduled at Fremantle General Hospital.

The conference was ambitious, bringing together renowned international speakers, clinicians, and practitioners from various fields of complementary medicine. It aimed to bridge traditional healing methods with modern medical practices–a concept that resonated deeply with my own experiences and aspirations.

Andrew, a seasoned professional, managed surgeries at both Willetton and Attadale, generously providing me with space to work at both locations. At Willetton, I was given an office, which became the administrative hub for the conference. In Attadale, he made a room available for me whenever he visited weekly, ensuring that I had access to the resources I needed to coordinate the event seamlessly.

Eager to infuse the conference with a touch of Sri Lankan culture, I approached Professor Jayasuriya with the idea, and he enthusiastically supported it. With Andrew's consent and the help of some Sri Lankan contacts in Perth, I reached out to the late Dr. Karunarathne, a well-respected community figure. When I explained my vision for the conference, he happily agreed to contribute, arranging for his two young children, Kanchana and Tara, to showcase traditional Sri Lankan drumming and Kandyan dancing during the opening ceremony.

Another integral cultural element I envisioned was a Sri Lankan traditional oil lamp, a symbol of light, knowledge, and auspicious beginnings. This lamp is typically lit during significant cultural and religious events in Sri Lanka. Mr. Ehalapola, a kind and generous community member, offered to provide the ceremonial lamp, adding a layer of authenticity and reverence to the occasion.

These contributions became much more than just performances or decorative additions; they were a bridge between my homeland and the professional world I was entering in Australia. They symbolised the richness of cultural heritage and the interconnectedness of global communities.

This chapter of my life, being in Australia, was just beginning, and though I missed my family deeply, I felt a sense of purpose and belonging in these new surroundings. The conference was shaping up to be not just an event but a landmark in my professional and personal journey.

Andrew was a lively, jovial character whose cheerful demeanour was infectious. Married with four children, he exuded a warmth that made anyone feel at home. From the very beginning, Andrew treated me not as an employee or an acquaintance but as a good friend. He often took me wherever he went, introducing me to his circle of friends, which included a mix of complementary health practitioners, doctors, and social acquaintances. Andrew had a knack for building bridges, and through him, I found myself welcomed into a new and vibrant social network.

Early on, Andrew decided to simplify my name for ease of reference and began calling me "Dr. Sam." The name caught on quickly, and soon, everyone around me, from colleagues to acquaintances, addressed me by this new moniker. It was a small gesture, but it helped me integrate into this new environment more seamlessly.

Andrew was not just a mentor in complementary medicine; he was also a great host, so going out for dinners and attending parties became a regular feature of life with him. He introduced me to the other doctors at his surgery, who were all welcoming and professional. While I could not see or treat patients due to my lack of Australian medical registration, I still found myself learning a great deal from observing and assisting Andrew in his medical centre whenever I was not occupied with conference-related tasks.

By that time, Andrew had already established his own school, Acupuncture Academy, where he trained medical colleagues in the art and science of acupuncture. Professor Jayasuriya, who had become a regular visitor to Australia, often served as a guest teacher for these sessions, which is how the two of them developed a strong friendship. My own training under Professor Jayasuriya had given me a solid foundation in acupuncture, and Andrew recognised this immediately. He encouraged me to join his classes as a co-teacher, allowing me to slowly ease into the role of an instructor. It was a great honour and a fulfilling experience to teach alongside Andrew while helping others develop their skills in acupuncture.

The international conference and accompanying workshops turned out to be a resounding success. The event brought together an eclectic mix of practitioners, experts, and enthusiasts from around the world.

Adapting to Australian life

Throughout my early days in Australia, I frequently encountered cultural nuances and linguistic differences that kept me on my toes. My attempts to adapt to Australian slang often resulted in humorous misunderstandings. For example, I vividly recall an instance when one of Dr. Ong's secretaries casually asked me, "How are you going?" Misinterpreting her question, I earnestly replied, "I'm taking the bus today." Her laughter made me realise that 'How are you going?" was not about my mode of transport but a casual way of asking how I was doing.

Similarly, when someone told me to "hang on," I found myself looking for something to hold on to until I finally understood its meaning, which is to say 'wait, I am not ready yet'. . These moments of confusion often turned into laughter, both for me and those around me. They became valuable lessons in navigating cultural differences with humour and humility, helping me settle into my new life in Australia.

Adjusting to life in Australia during those initial months was both a learning curve and an adventure. When I went shopping for essentials like bread and bananas, I could not help but convert the prices into Sri Lankan rupees. The disparity was striking, and I often hesitated, wondering if I really needed that loaf of bread or a bunch of bananas. The habit of mentally converting currency made even the simplest purchase feel monumental. However, as the weeks turned into months, I adapted, realising that the cost of living was just a part of the new reality I was embracing.

Navigating social customs was another area where I encountered a few amusing missteps. On one occasion, I went out to dinner with the staff from the surgery. In Sri Lanka, it was customary for the host to cover the bill, so I naturally assumed that the person who invited us would pay for everyone. Imagine my surprise when the bill was divided among all the attendees! It was an eye-opening moment, and though I felt a little awkward, it became one of the many lessons I learned about Australian culture.

Another memorable experience was attending a Bring Your Own (BYO) dinner. Not knowing much about Australian drinking customs, I brought a bottle of port wine, which I happily began drinking during the meal. It was only later that I realised port wine is typically a dessert wine meant to be enjoyed after the meal rather than during it. Although I was initially embarrassed, it spurred me to learn more about wines, and I eventually took a wine appreciation course, which not only expanded my knowledge but also kindled a lifelong enjoyment of fine wines.

Adapting to humour and social interactions also brought its share of surprises. A few times, colleagues or acquaintances made comments that I found offensive. However, they would quickly follow up with, "I'm only joking," lightening the mood and teaching me that humour in Australia often has a sharp, playful edge. Emboldened by this, I attempted to joke in the same manner, but my efforts were met with puzzled looks or silence rather than laughter. I realised that mastering humour in a new cultural context was a skill in itself!

One of the quirks of Australian culture I encountered was the ubiquitous greeting, "G'day mate, how are you going?" At first, I thought the strangers greeting me had mistaken me for someone they knew. It took me some time to understand that this was a friendly, everyday way of saying hello. I even tried using this phrase once when stopped by a police officer conducting a random alcohol check. Despite my attempt to sound casual and blend in, it did not work as I had hoped–the officer remained entirely professional, though I like to think I amused him a little!

Social gatherings and parties hosted by my brother-in-law's friends were a constant source of camaraderie and joy. Many of them were Sri Lankan students in Australia studying various vocational and higher education courses, and they treated me with great respect, calling me "Aiya" (brother) in a way that made me feel at home. Their warmth and hospitality helped ease the transition into this new chapter of my life, making those early days far less daunting. These gatherings were not just about food and drinks; they were moments that solidified friendships and reminded me that even in a foreign land, the bonds of culture and community could create a sense of belonging.

Although I enjoyed the hospitality of my brother-in-law and his friends, I often missed my wife and children deeply. I called them whenever I could and wrote letters to my wife, as email and free communication options like WhatsApp were not available back then. As soon as I got my visa extended, I arranged the necessary paperwork and submitted it to the department of immigration to enable my wife and children to apply for a visiting visa.

Navigating life in a new country sometimes meant facing challenging and humbling moments. One such incident still lingers in my memory as a lesson learned the hard way. After attending a lively party with some friends, everyone departed separately. I found myself alone, left to navigate my way back home. Unfortunately, I was intoxicated and unfamiliar with the roads. The situation was compounded by the lack of navigation apps or tools that could have guided me in those days.

Feeling increasingly disoriented, I did the only sensible thing I could think of: I called Sam, a friend of my brother-in-law, and explained my predicament. Using the fragmented directions I could provide for my location, he managed to locate me and guide me home safely. The experience was a sobering one, both literally and figuratively. I was grateful for Sam's assistance and vowed never to repeat such a mistake again, a promise I have kept to this day.

During my first year in Australia, my brother-in-law Nandaka and his wife graciously took care of me, providing food, accommodations, and a sense of familial support that was invaluable. Their kindness created a foundation of stability as I adjusted to life in a new country, away from my wife and children.

Laying down roots

As the international conference concluded successfully, Andrew recognised my contributions and commitment. He took the initiative to sponsor an extension of my visa for another three years, citing plans for clinical trials and teaching projects. The visa, which included working rights, marked a turning point for me, solidifying my role at his academy and clinic and allowing me to fully immerse myself in the work. The proximity of the academy to his surgery in Willetton made it easy to integrate clinical trials, data recording, and teaching into a seamless operation

Andrew's Acupuncture Academy became a hub of activity and learning. I assisted him in his clinics, helped train medical professionals in the art of acupuncture, and even taught some of the courses offered at his academy. Occasionally, after consultations, doctors would ask me to administer acupuncture treatments, allowing me to refine my skills further. This hands-on experience and collaboration were immensely rewarding and gave me a deeper appreciation for the therapeutic potential of acupuncture.

With Andrew's guidance, I was introduced to a network of medical professionals and practitioners. He frequently invited me to join him at medical seminars, workshops, and meetings, where he introduced me to his colleagues. These events were not only opportunities to learn but also platforms to establish connections within the medical community in Western Australia. Andrew's unwavering belief in my abilities and his efforts to create opportunities for me helped me carve out a space for myself in this unfamiliar professional landscape.

These early experiences were instrumental in laying the groundwork for my medical and personal future in Australia. They were not just about professional development: they were about building confidence, trust, and a sense of belonging. Through challenges, collaborations, and moments of discovery, I began to see Australia not just as a temporary place of residence but as a land where I could envision a future for myself and my family.

The moment I received the news that my wife and two children were granted visas to join me in Australia, I was overcome with a sense of exhilaration and fulfilment. The separation had been difficult, so the thought of reuniting with my family filled me with immense joy. They arrived in the middle of 1991, and seeing their faces at the airport remains one of the most heartwarming memories of my life.

Initially, we stayed with my brother-in-law and his family in Booragoon, sharing a house that was bustling with warmth and familial bonds. This arrangement provided a stable beginning as we navigated our new life together. After a few months, however, we decided to move into our own space and rented a modest two-bedroom unit in Lynwood. While it was not an ideal environment for raising a young family, it served as a stepping-stone toward building our future. Our two children started attending Lynwood Primary School, marking their first experience of the Australian education system.

In January 1992, with careful financial planning, we took the leap and purchased our first property in Australia–a significant milestone in our journey. The house, located on High Road in Riverton, was a three-bedroom, one-bathroom home with a spacious patio and a swimming pool. It cost us $81,176, with a mortgage payment of $358 every fortnight at an interest rate of 9.95%. Owning a home brought us a sense of pride and stability, though the swimming pool, while initially exciting, quickly became more of a chore than a luxury. Most weekends, I found myself cleaning it rather than using it, as my wife and children rarely ventured into the water.

Not long after their arrival, my wife became pregnant with our third child, Kalpana. For her care, I entrusted Dr. Ng, one of my acupuncture students who was also an accomplished obstetrician. Dr Ng's expertise and compassionate approach reassured us throughout the pregnancy.

In line with my growing belief in holistic and complementary medicine, we decided to have the delivery managed with acupuncture rather than relying on traditional anaesthetics or strong painkillers. The delivery took place at Swan District Hospital, where Dr. Ng operated. On the day of delivery, I personally administered acupuncture to my wife to manage her pain and facilitate the process. The birth was uneventful, and both mother and baby were alert and cheerful immediately after the delivery. My wife later remarked that this experience was far more positive compared to her earlier deliveries, with fewer side effects and a quicker recovery. This event further cemented my faith in acupuncture as a viable and effective medical practice in certain conditions.

While I worked tirelessly, often seven days a week, my wife proved to be the cornerstone of our family. She managed the household with remarkable efficiency, ensuring our expenses were carefully balanced against my modest salary. We led a simple lifestyle, avoiding extravagant purchases or dining out at restaurants. Our meals were wholesome and home-cooked, a reflection of her ability to stretch every dollar while ensuring our family's needs were met.

At this stage, our social circle was small, comprising only of a handful of Sri Lankan families. However, our neighbours, a friendly Italian family, were warm and welcoming, making us feel part of the local community.

My first car in Australia was a used Holden Commodore, purchased in 1991 on the recommendation of an Australian friend. The car served us well, providing reliable transportation for a year before I upgraded to a brand-new Ford Falcon in 1992. The Falcon symbolised a new chapter of growth and confidence in our ability to establish ourselves in this foreign land.

The early years in Australia were a time of hard work, sacrifice, and resilience. Despite the challenges, we were united as a family, driven by shared goals and aspirations. Every step, from buying our first home to welcoming our third child, reinforced our determination to build a better future. These experiences not only strengthened our bond as a family but also deepened my appreciation for the opportunities and lessons that come with starting anew in a different country.

Birth of the Acupuncture Association of Australia, New Zealand, and Asia (AAANZA)

A new association was to emerge soon into my life. The idea to create a professional body that would represent acupuncturists across Australia, New Zealand, and Asia was born from Andrew's visionary thinking. He believed in bringing together medical doctors and non-medical practitioners who had studied acupuncture through his academy into a single, cohesive organisation. This body aimed to elevate the practice of acupuncture, foster collaboration among practitioners, and advocate for professional recognition in the region.

The organisation was named the Acupuncture Association of Australia, New Zealand, and Asia (AAANZA), reflecting its broad geographic focus and commitment to inclusivity. Andrew was unanimously elected as the chairman, and I was honoured to serve as the secretary. At the time, the acupuncture landscape in Australia was fragmented, with two main professional bodies already established. One was based in the eastern states and had a significant membership of non-medical acupuncturists; the other was the Australian Medical Acupuncture Society (AMAS), a group exclusively composed of medical professionals. AMAS provided acupuncture training courses strictly for doctors, reinforcing a division between medically trained and non-medically trained practitioners.

However, the existence of these two well-established acupuncture organisations presented a significant challenge to the incorporation of

AAANZA. The regulators questioned the necessity of forming another body and expressed concerns about potential overlaps and conflicts. However, Andrew's unwavering determination proved to be the driving force behind AAANZA's eventual success. Andrew's relentless nature and his ability to persevere through obstacles were inspiring. He refused to accept rejection, wrote letters, provided evidence, and engaged in dialogue with the regulators until they finally approved the incorporation of AAANZA in 1992. His efforts taught me an invaluable lesson: Perseverance can transform impossibility into achievement.

AAANZA set out to provide a platform that was inclusive and forward-thinking, welcoming both medical doctors and non-doctors who had been trained in acupuncture. This inclusivity distinguished the organisation from others and allowed for a more diverse and comprehensive representation of the acupuncture community. Through its initiatives, AAANZA created opportunities for education, networking, and advocacy, helping to elevate the profile of acupuncture in Australia and beyond.

Being part of the creation of AAANZA was a deeply fulfilling experience for me. It not only allowed me to contribute to the advancement of acupuncture but also offered insights into leadership, collaboration, and the art of persistence. Working closely with Andrew, I learned that vision and grit could overcome even the most formidable challenges. The journey to establish AAANZA marked a pivotal chapter in my professional life, one that would lay the groundwork for many future endeavours in the field of complementary medicine.

In 1991, under Andrew's dynamic stewardship, the Acupuncture Academy of Australia, in collaboration with the Australian Institute of Holistic Medicine, which had not yet been incorporated, and the Acupuncture Association of Australia, New Zealand, and Asia

(AAANZA) organised an International Seminar on Acupuncture and Holistic Medicine in Kuala Lumpur, Malaysia. This was a significant milestone, as it brought together practitioners and enthusiasts of complementary medicine from Australia, Malaysia, and other parts of the world. The seminar was held from 6 to November 9, 1991, at the prestigious Concord Hotel in Kuala Lumpur. It attracted an impressive turnout of participants, including seasoned professionals and emerging voices in acupuncture and holistic medicine. For me, this was not just another professional engagement but an enriching experience that allowed me to witness the global perspective on complementary medicine. It underscored the importance of collaboration and cultural exchange in advancing the acupuncture field.

While the seminar days were packed with learning, presentations, and discussions, the evenings were reserved for camaraderie and cultural immersion. The organisers and local delegates ensured we experienced the famed Malaysian hospitality. Every night, we were treated to parties and social gatherings that showcased local cuisine, traditions, and a spirit of togetherness. These informal events were as impactful as the formal sessions, as they fostered meaningful connections and built friendships that transcended professional boundaries.

The balance of intellectual stimulation during the day and lively social interactions at night made this event truly memorable. This seminar became my second firsthand experience in organising and participating in an international conference, and it deepened my appreciation for the global reach and potential of complementary medicine.

Becoming a subject of a test case: Is acupuncture a medical practice?

Sometime in October 1991, I received a letter from the Registrar of the Medical Board of Western Australia, and its contents marked the beginning of a challenging and defining chapter in my professional life. The letter sought details about my work at the Acupuncture Academy, which was connected with the surgery run by Andrew, and questioned the nature of my job, the scope of my activities, and what entitled me to use the title "Doctor" in Western Australia.

This inquiry initially seemed routine, but it soon became clear that it was the result of a formal complaint lodged against me. I responded promptly and transparently, explaining that I was employed at the academy to teach, conduct research on the efficacy of acupuncture, and train doctors in the art of acupuncture. I justified my use of the title "Doctor" based on my PhD in acupuncture and made it clear that I was not practising as a medical doctor in Western Australia.

Despite my response, the situation escalated, leaving me puzzled about the source of the complaint. It seemed likely that someone had acted out of professional jealousy, unhappy with the growing prominence of Andrew's Academy or my role within it. Another possibility was that the complaint originated from the Australian Medical Acupuncture Society (AMAS), which exclusively trained and credentialed doctors in acupuncture. Andrew had been a member of this society before leaving to establish his own academy, citing dissatisfaction with how the society operated.

By April or May 1992, matters had taken a serious turn. I was served a summons issued by the Magistrate Court of Western Australia on behalf of the Medical Board. The charges levelled against me were as follows:

Using the title "Dr" contrary to Section 19(2) of the Medical Act 1894, as I was not a registered medical practitioner in Western Australia. Holding myself out as willing to perform a medical service contrary to Section 19(3) of the Medical Act 1894, alleging that acupuncture was a medical service and thus only permissible for registered medical practitioners to provide. The Medical Board claimed that acupuncture constituted a medical service and that only registered medical practitioners in Western Australia were authorised to provide it. These charges were rooted in a legal framework established under the Medical Act 1894. This antiquated legislation no longer reflected the contemporary landscape of healthcare practices like acupuncture. Fortunately, by 2010, the Health Practitioner Regulation National Law (WA) Act replaced this outdated Medical Act, rendering many of its clauses obsolete. However, this older law still applied at the time of the charges in 1992.

I carefully reviewed the court documents, repeatedly scrutinising them to understand the charges and determine if there had been any misunderstanding and could not recall performing any service that contravened Western Australian law. I had previously received a letter from the Medical Board requesting clarification of my qualifications and activities at the academy, to which I had responded. However, I received no feedback or follow-up to that initial correspondence and believed the matter had been resolved.

I got a copy of the Medical Act 1894 and tried to understand the relevant section of the Act, though that was somewhat challenging. Section 19 of the Act stated:

From and after the passing of this Act, no person other than a medical practitioner shall be entitled to

(1) practise medicine or surgery in all or any one or more of its branches; or to

(2) advertise or hold himself out as being, or in any manner to pretend to be, or to take or use the name or title, (alone or in conjunction with any other title, word, or letter) of a physician, doctor of medicine, licentiate in medicine or surgery, master in surgery, bachelor of medicine or surgery, doctor, surgeon, medical qualified or registered practitioner, apothecary, accoucheur, or any other medical or surgical name or title, or to

(3) advertise or hold himself out, directly or indirectly, by any name, word, title or designation, whether expressed in words or by letters or partly in the one and partly in the other (either alone or in conjunction with any other word or words) or by any other means whatsoever, as being entitled or qualified, able, or willing or by implication suggests that he is able or willing or in any manner pretends to practise medicine or surgery in any one or more of its or their branches or to give or perform any medical or surgical service, attendance, operation or advice or any service, attendance, operation or advice which is usually given or performed by a medical practitioner.

Later, I realised this Act's extensive restrictions and limitations prevented many health practitioners and other professionals from performing their tasks or using their titles effectively.

The summons brought an overwhelming sense of uncertainty and helplessness. I had never encountered legal proceedings or court documents of this nature in my life. The prospect of defending myself against a formal complaint from a regulatory body seemed daunting and fraught with potential consequences. I informed Andrew about the situation, but the details of his immediate reaction have faded from my memory. What I do remember vividly is the support and encouragement he provided as the events unfolded. Andrew believed in my integrity and the value of the work we were doing at the academy.

As the details of the case emerged, I learned that the charges stemmed from a visit by a private investigator posing as a patient and hired by the Medical Board of Western Australia. It became apparent that this was a test case, orchestrated to challenge the practice of acupuncture in Western Australia.

The complaint highlighted the tensions between conventional medicine and complementary therapies, as well as between those who viewed acupuncture as a standalone practice and those who believed it should remain under the exclusive purview of medical practitioners.

As the court date in August 1992 approached, I sought legal counsel to mount a defence. My lawyer informed me that the charges stemmed from an acupuncture session conducted in March 1992 at the Pinetree Gully Surgery, where I had treated a patient named Paul Scott. This incident had been orchestrated by the Medical Board, which hired a private investigator to pose as a patient under a false name and submit a complaint. I found this revelation unsettling but not entirely surprising. The Medical Board seemed intent on framing a legal case against me, specifically targeting my practice of acupuncture and the use of the title "Doctor." It became clear that this was a test case, with implications extending beyond my personal situation to broader issues surrounding the regulation of acupuncture in Australia.

Despite the allegations, I knew I had acted within the boundaries of my role at the academy and began gathering evidence to demonstrate that acupuncture was widely practised by non-medical practitioners across Australia. The Yellow Pages directory listed numerous individuals providing acupuncture services who were not registered medical practitioners. Additionally, the academy had strict protocols ensuring that any acupuncture administered at the clinic was done under the supervision of licensed doctors.

This legal challenge was more than a personal struggle; it was a test case that reflected broader debates about the legitimacy of complementary medicine and the regulatory framework governing it. While I felt the weight of the charges, I was determined to defend not only my integrity but also the validity of acupuncture as a respected practice accessible to both medical and non-medical practitioners. The case also underscored the need for clarity and fairness in the regulation of complementary therapies, a mission that would continue to shape my journey in Australia for many years.

My lawyer and I prepared a detailed defence highlighting the educational and research-based nature of my role. Andrew also offered his full support, providing testimony to clarify that I had never misrepresented myself as a medical practitioner and that acupuncture, as practised in the academy, was not exclusively a medical service.

In the days leading up to the court hearing, I delved into research, uncovering numerous advertisements in the Yellow Pages for acupuncture services offered by non-medical practitioners across Western Australia. This bolstered my belief that I had not violated any laws. The doctors at the surgery, including Andrew, reassured me that my actions were entirely within legal boundaries. They emphasised that acupuncture was not limited to registered medical practitioners and that my role at the academy fell well within the law.

The case was scheduled for August 7, 1992, at the Magistrate Court in Perth. My lawyer entered a not-guilty plea on my behalf for both charges. The courtroom was charged with tension, as the case was one of the first of its kind, testing the interpretation of acupuncture as a medical service and the use of professional titles in Western Australia.

The Medical Board's lawyer presented Dr. K, the President of the Australian Medical Acupuncture Society (AMAS), as an expert witness. Dr. K was both a medical practitioner and an acupuncturist, with a personal stake in positioning acupuncture as a service exclusive to the medical profession. Dr. K's testimony was central to the prosecution's case, and he described AMAS as a national organisation committed to promoting the "proper use of acupuncture among medical practitioners." He admitted that full membership was restricted to medical practitioners, but the association allowed dentists and veterinary surgeons to join as associate members. Interestingly, he acknowledged that he had obtained his acupuncture qualifications through the very association he now presided over.

During his testimony, Dr. K emphasised that acupuncture was primarily used to treat painful conditions and that it was often administered in conjunction with conventional Western medicine. He then argued that acupuncture should be classified as a medical service, pointing to the existence of a Medicare item number that allowed patients to claim rebates for acupuncture treatments provided by medical practitioners.

Interestingly, Dr. K's cross-examination by my solicitor revealed some contradictions in his arguments. Specifically, he asked questions about acupuncture training and alternative medicine, among others.

Training in Acupuncture: When asked if acupuncture was part of his medical degree, Dr. K admitted it was not. He agreed that acupuncture was not included in the medical curriculum in Australia or Western

Australia, highlighting that it required two hundred hours of postgraduate learning to acquire basic proficiency.

Complementary Medicine: My lawyer questioned Dr K's statement about combining acupuncture with Western medicine, suggesting that this implied acupuncture was a complementary therapy rather than a strictly medical service. Dr. K agreed, acknowledging that acupuncture could serve as an alternative when Western medicine fell short.

Inviting Experts: Dr K admitted that AMAS invited international experts in acupuncture to conduct seminars and workshops in Australia, many of whom were not registered medical practitioners in the country. He further conceded that these experts were often addressed as "Doctor" out of respect for their qualifications in their home countries.

Professional Affiliation: Dr. K confirmed that AMAS was affiliated with the Australian Medical Association (AMA) and that medical practitioners often referred patients to him for acupuncture treatments, underscoring his expertise in the field.

The cross-examination exposed the ambiguities and inconsistencies in the Medical Board's stance. It became clear that acupuncture was neither universally recognised as a medical service nor exclusively practised by medical practitioners.

Then, the private investigator, hired by the Medical Board of Western Australia, took the stand during the hearing. Posing as a patient, his role had been pivotal in initiating the legal proceedings. Under cross-examination, the investigator detailed his visit to the clinic, recounting how he had sought acupuncture treatment under false pretences. His testimony aimed to establish that I had allegedly misrepresented myself as a doctor. However, my lawyer skillfully dismantled the credibility of his claims, highlighting the deceitful nature of his role and the Board's intention to frame a case against me.

Andrew's testimony was the cornerstone of my defence. As a registered medical practitioner in Western Australia and a qualified acupuncturist, his credibility was undeniable. He had trained under the renowned Professor Anton Jayasuriya, the same mentor who had taught me the art and science of acupuncture. When questioned about acupuncture's inclusion in medical curricula, Andrew made it unequivocally clear:

"Acupuncture is not part of the standard medical curriculum in Australia."

He elaborated that many medical professionals in Australia viewed acupuncture as an invalid therapeutic modality, often dismissing it as "mambo-jumbo." However, he firmly argued that this perception was unjustified, as acupuncture had been proven effective in numerous cases.

Andrew emphasised my role as a consultant in acupuncture, explaining that I operated under a valid work permit, assisting doctors in their practice and teaching acupuncture through the academy. Addressing the charge that acupuncture constituted a "medical service," he drew an insightful analogy: "It's like saying that spinal manipulation should only be performed by doctors when we know chiropractors do it daily." His point underscored that acupuncture, like chiropractic care, was widely practised by non-medical professionals across Australia.

Andrew's frustration with the Medical Board of Western Australia was palpable. He revealed that the Board prohibited registered medical practitioners from displaying their acupuncture qualifications, a move that contradicted their stance that acupuncture was a medical service. Andrew described this as a "double standard," lamenting that:

"On one hand, we don't believe in acupuncture; on the other, we don't allow others to practice it. It's a contradiction that embarrasses the medical profession.'

Andrew passionately defended my work, stating that I had never represented myself as a medical practitioner and had always practised under the supervision of registered doctors. He also noted that less than 5 percent of medical practitioners in Australia practised acupuncture, highlighting its status as a specialised and often undervalued field.

The courtroom fell silent as the magistrate delivered his verdict. He acknowledged the ambiguity in the legal framework surrounding acupuncture and its regulation in Western Australia. In his remarks, he stated:

"Mr. Jayawardana does possess medical qualifications obtained in Sri Lanka, but these are not recognised in Western Australia. He appears to be practising in a specialised field, acupuncture, in which he holds impeccable qualifications. This case represents a technical breach of the law, not a substantive one."

The magistrate dismissed the charge of holding oneself out as being willing to perform a medical service (contrary to section 19(3) of the Medical Act 1894). However, the charge of using the title "Doctor" without registration (section 19(2)) was proven. Despite this, the magistrate chose to dismiss the charge under section 669(1)(a) of the Criminal Code, noting: "It seems a shame that someone with such qualifications should face conviction over a technicality."

The outcome was bittersweet; while I avoided a conviction, the case highlighted the bureaucratic hurdles faced by professionals in emerging fields like acupuncture. The judgment garnered widespread media attention, portraying it as an instance of bureaucratic overreach and injustice. News outlets portrayed the case as emblematic of the challenges faced by professionals in complementary medicine, especially those with foreign qualifications navigating Australia's rigid systems. While the media attention brought me some measure of comfort, it also highlighted the broader issue of regulatory frameworks failing to accommodate emerging disciplines like acupuncture.

The legal battle came at a significant cost as well–both financially and emotionally. The defence expenses amounted to a daunting sum for someone still building a life in a new country. Yet, I was overwhelmed by the generosity of friends and supporters, both practitioners and enthusiasts of complementary medicine, who rallied behind me, offering both financial and moral support. Their kindness reminded me of the power of community during adversity. This outpouring of overwhelming support is one of the most heartening aspects of this ordeal. The encouragement, solidarity, and advocacy of my colleagues and friends made me feel less isolated in one of my life's most difficult periods.

This legal episode became a defining moment in my journey, solidifying my resolve to advocate for fair and inclusive regulations in complementary medicine. It reinforced my belief that every challenge, no matter how daunting, can be an opportunity for growth and positive change. At the same time, I recognised the ongoing risks of continuing my work at the Surgery and Academy under the existing regulatory framework. The experience also illuminated the importance of establishing clear guidelines and protections for those practising complementary medicine, ensuring that others would not have to endure similar trials as I had.

CHAPTER 6
Striving for Excellence in My Professional and Personal Lives

By 1992, my professional journey had gained momentum, and significant changes were on the horizon. While working at Andrew's Acupuncture Academy of Australia, I actively trained doctors and administered acupuncture. During this period, we noticed a growing interest among people looking for alternative career paths or avenues for professional development. This interest sparked the idea of offering complementary medicine courses, which Andrew quickly embraced.

Together, we decided to establish a new business, the Australian Institute of Holistic Medicine, which aimed to offer structured education in various complementary therapies. At the time, my knowledge of complementary medicine was limited, so we enlisted the help of colleagues in Perth practising complementary medicine. Their expertise became instrumental in designing the curriculum and delivering the courses.

The inaugural course was a six-month program that included foundational subjects such as anatomy and physiology, medical terminology, and naturopathic nutrition. The classes were held in the evenings at Andrew's academy, a small teaching facility adjacent to his surgery.

Even as the course progressed, I made it a point to deepen my understanding of complementary medicine. I researched similar courses offered in Australia and discovered that many were recognised by associations set up by college owners, particularly in the eastern states.

These programs often included three-year diploma courses in naturopathy, structured with longer breaks between terms or semesters. However, there were no national regulations governing the practice of complementary medicine in Australia at the time, leaving the field self-regulated by professional associations.

Launching the Australian Institute of Holistic Medicine marked a pivotal moment in my career, creating an opportunity to contribute to an evolving field while bridging the gap between traditional and modern healing practices. The experience taught me invaluable lessons about innovation, perseverance, and the power of education in transforming lives.

In 1992, we had only seven students enrolled in our complementary medicine courses, which we continued to offer over the weekends. It was a modest beginning, but it marked the foundation of something much more significant. Despite the small numbers, the courses symbolised a pioneering step toward formalised training in complementary medicine in Australia, a field still emerging and often misunderstood.

Significant changes in the training and education landscape

The early 1990s saw major developments in vocational education and training in Australia, profoundly influencing my journey in complementary medicine education. Among these developments was the establishment of the State Employment and Skills Development Authority (SESDA), a pivotal moment for education and training providers in Western Australia. SESDA was created to register and approve skills formation agencies that delivered accredited programs under the SESDA Act.

On December 1, 1993, SESDA was amalgamated with the Department of Employment, Vocational Education, and Training (DEVET) to form the Western Australian Department of Training. It provided an opportunity to elevate the status of complementary medicine education. While complementary medicine was unregulated, SESDA and, later, the Department of Training established pathways to offer recognised and accredited training. These frameworks allowed us to begin envisioning a three-year Diploma of Natural Medicine, aligning our courses with state-approved standards and giving students a tangible qualification recognised by professional associations.

This era of change offered both challenges and opportunities. The evolving regulatory landscape encouraged innovation in course design while ensuring that training met the expectations of students and industries. These systems gave credibility to our work, and although our beginnings were humble, we were laying the foundation for what would become a recognised educational institution in complementary medicine.

Reflecting on this period, it is clear that the intersection of personal growth and systemic change provided a fertile ground for progress. While complementary medicine remained self-regulated, the frameworks established during this time created the infrastructure necessary for its gradual recognition as a legitimate field of practice.

In 1993, we reached a significant milestone by finalising and submitting our three-year Diploma in Natural Medicine for approval. Thankfully, this course was subsequently approved and recognised by the regulatory body in Western Australia, a major achievement for us and for complementary medicine education. At that time, vocational education in Australia lacked a unified national framework, and each state managed and regulated its own vocational training programs independently.

The field of complementary medicine was still in its infancy when it came to formal regulation, as no regulatory body existed then (and still does not exist today) to oversee the practice of complementary medicine or its practitioners in Australia. Instead, the industry relied on self-regulation through professional associations, which set their own standards and guidelines for practice. While these associations provided some structure, the lack of legislative oversight meant that complementary medicine practitioners faced challenges in gaining widespread professional recognition.

An interesting exception to the unregulated status of complementary medicine occurred in the Northern Territory (NT) during the late 1980s and early 1990s. The NT was the only Australian jurisdiction to mandate statutory registration for naturopaths, a progressive step that offered practitioners professional credibility and legal recognition. This system attracted practitioners from other states who sought registration to boost their standing within the profession.

However, this era of regulation in the NT was short-lived. The introduction of the Mutual Recognition Act 1992, which facilitated the recognition of professional qualifications across Australian states and territories, dismantled the NT's unique naturopath registration system. As a result, naturopathy reverted to being an unregistered profession across the country, a status that remains unchanged to this day. This development underscored the fragmented nature of complementary medicine regulation in Australia during that period, posing challenges for practitioners seeking consistent professional acknowledgement.

In 1993, our institution took a formal step forward when the Australian Institute of Holistic Medicine (AIHM) became an incorporated company limited by guarantee. This new structure gave us a solid foundation to grow our operations, attract students, and gain academic and professional credibility. The organisation also became a Registered Training Organisation (RTO) in 1993.

Andrew and I both became directors of the company, and I assumed the additional responsibility of serving as the secretary. Incorporation brought a new level of professionalism and accountability to our endeavours, signalling our commitment to providing high-quality education and fostering a legitimate path for complementary medicine practitioners.

The incorporation of AIHM aligned with broader efforts to bring structure and recognition to the field of complementary medicine. By offering a three-year Diploma in Natural Medicine, we aimed to create a comprehensive, credible curriculum that met the educational needs of aspiring practitioners while adhering to the regulatory standards of the time. This period was one of determination and vision. Despite the challenges posed by a fragmented regulatory environment, we laid the groundwork for a future where complementary medicine could thrive as a respected and recognised profession.

It was time to expand, evolve, and embrace change. The vision was clear: establish a dedicated education campus that would offer a physical space for learning and a nurturing environment for students and faculty to thrive. The move was not merely about scaling up but about creating an institution that reflected my passion for holistic education and my unwavering commitment to complementary medicine.

The decision to leave Andrew's premises was not easy. The memories, the struggles, and the victories within those walls had become a part of my identity. However, growth often demands stepping out of one's comfort zone. So, with renewed determination, I set out to find a location that would accommodate a larger student body, provide state-of-the-art facilities, and offer a conducive environment for innovation in education.

The search led to a new campus, a space with potential and possibilities. This was not just a geographical move; it symbolised a turning point in my journey, both personally and professionally. The challenges ahead were daunting: building a campus from scratch, attracting new students, and ensuring the quality of education remained impeccable. But the excitement of creating something transformative outweighed the fears.

I was leaving behind a chapter that had given me so much: Andrew's unwavering support, the camaraderie of my colleagues, and the foundation of an educational legacy. But I carried with me the lessons learned, the friendships forged, and a relentless drive to make the next phase even more impactful. The setup at Andrew's Academy, though functional, was not conducive to my vision of what education could be. I dreamed of creating a space where students could thrive, where education was not just about knowledge but about transformation. But dreams require a foundation, and for me, that meant finding the right property to establish a proper college.

Building a dream

The next chapter of my life would unfold within the walls of this new campus, where dreams would be realised and new challenges embraced. What hurdles would I face in this uncharted territory? How would the vision of a holistic education institution take shape? Would this leap of faith lead to success, or would it present unforeseen trials?

This move marked the beginning of an exciting yet uncertain journey, one that would test my resolve and redefine the boundaries of what I believed was possible. The story of the new campus is not just about brick and mortar: it is about building a dream, shaping lives, and navigating the highs and lows of progress.

The search for a suitable property was difficult. Financially, I faced significant limitations because I did not have enough savings to make the required deposit for a mortgage. It was during this time that Andrew stepped forward with incredible generosity and mortgaged one of his properties to secure a loan from Bankwest, allowing us to proceed with the purchase. His faith in my vision and partnership gave me the courage to take this leap.

In 1994, we found a property in Cockburn Central, a 2½-acre plot of land with a modest house. The house had three bedrooms, one bathroom, and two toilets. While it was not perfect, it had potential. I saw in it the foundation of a dream waiting to be realised. The settlement occurred on November 25, 1994, marking a significant milestone in my journey.

The property, though promising, required extensive modifications to transform it into a functional educational facility. Funds were tight, and hiring professional builders was out of the question. The responsibility of making this vision a reality fell squarely on my shoulders, but I was determined to do whatever was necessary to make it work.

One of my closest friends, Benny, stepped in to help. Together, we tackled the challenge of converting the living room into a lecture hall. It was hard work and not without its mishaps. I remember vividly the day we tried to remove some of the columns at the entrance to the living room, and a small misstep almost caused the wall to collapse. My heart raced as I realised how close we had come to disaster. With quick thinking and teamwork, we managed to anchor the structure and prevent further damage. That day taught me a valuable lesson about perseverance and resourcefulness.

The financial burden of the project was significant. We had borrowed the entire amount needed to purchase the property, using it as security, along with one of Andrew's properties. This created immense pressure to generate enough income to cover not only my wages and outgoings but also the monthly mortgage payments. It was a heavy load to carry, but I was unwavering in my commitment to succeed.

The first intake of students arrived soon after we completed the initial modifications. To my astonishment, the demand far exceeded our expectations. We had forty students enrolled, more than the space could comfortably accommodate. One student, unable to find a seat, made a heartfelt plea. She said she did not mind standing if she could be part of the course. Her determination was infectious; it reignited my energy and enthusiasm, reminding me why I had embarked on this journey in the first place.

The college's early days were far from glamorous, but they were filled with purpose. The property, though simple and modest, became a place of learning, growth, and transformation. Every financial, structural, or logistical challenge became a stepping-stone toward something greater.

This chapter of my life was not just about building a college: it was about building resilience, learning to trust in the kindness and support of others, and staying true to a vision despite the odds. The students' determination, the generosity of friends like Benny and Andrew, and my unwavering resolve made it possible to turn a dream into reality.

Despite the initial challenges and difficulties, those early days in Cockburn Central were not just the beginning of a college but the foundation of a legacy. Adversity has always been a silent teacher in my life, shaping me in ways that I could never have anticipated. Each challenge brought with it an opportunity to grow stronger, to become more determined, and to find something good even in the hardest of times.

In 1994, I decided to enhance my knowledge and skills in teaching to provide greater value to my students. With this goal in mind, I enrolled in the Graduate Diploma in Education program at Curtin University in Perth, which I successfully completed in 1996. This qualification proved invaluable, equipping me with the expertise needed to design and develop future courses at the Australian Institute of Holistic Medicine. It also significantly improved the effectiveness of course delivery, ensuring a more enriching learning experience for students.

The building of a real estate portfolio

By 1993, my family and I had reached a pivotal moment: We received our Australian permanent residency. The sense of relief and joy was profound. This was not just a piece of paper but a gateway to stability, freedom, and a brighter future.

The year 1994 was a crucial one in my journey as a property investor, marking the first time I experienced the tangible rewards of real estate. We sold our first property on High Road, Riverton, for $105,432, making a profit of $20,000. It may not seem like a staggering amount, but to us, it represented the potential of real estate to create wealth. This success laid the foundation for our future endeavours and gave us the confidence to take our next steps.

With the proceeds, my wife and I purchased a plot of land in Canning Vale for $64,000 and built our first family home, a four-by-two house with a study for $75,000. The construction was undertaken by Plunkett Home Builders, and I recall the immense satisfaction of watching our vision come to life. This house was not just bricks and mortar; it was a symbol of stability and progress. For five years, we made it our sanctuary, filled with memories and milestones.

While the Canning Vale house served as our family home, the success and smooth functioning of this phase of life were due to the remarkable efforts of my wife. A trained quantity surveyor and an intelligent, capable woman, she managed the home front with extraordinary efficiency, leaving me available to focus on my work.

At the time, I was engaged almost seven days a week, building my professional career and working tirelessly to ensure our financial stability. While I was deeply involved in these endeavours, my wife took on the responsibility of driving our children to Willetton twice a day to attend school, as it was outside the Canning Vale area. In addition, she ensured they participated in extracurricular activities, nurturing their development and providing them with opportunities that would shape their future.

Her contributions extended beyond logistics and child-rearing. My wife also managed the reticulation and garden of our Canning Vale home with great care, transforming it into a space of beauty and comfort. Together, we also undertook the tiling of the house as a cost-saving measure, spending weekends and evenings working side by side. These shared projects were not just practical; they were bonding experiences that reminded me of the strength of our partnership.

My wife's unwavering support and ability to manage every aspect of the household gave me the peace of mind to focus on my professional pursuits. Knowing that everything at home was running smoothly was a gift I deeply valued. Her contributions during this period were nothing short of extraordinary and formed a cornerstone of our family's success.

As our family grew, so did our aspirations, particularly when it came to our children's education. Education had always been a cornerstone of my values, and I wanted my children to have the best opportunities possible. This led us to move to Rhonda Avenue in Willetton, purchasing a modest three-bedroom, one-bathroom home for approximately $120,000. The move was strategic, placing us within the school zone of Rossmoyne Senior High School, one of the top state government schools at the time.

While relocating meant leaving behind our beloved Canning Vale home, we decided to retain it as a rental property. The rental income covered its mortgage, making it a sound financial decision and marking the beginning of a more structured approach to real estate, combining personal needs with investment strategies.

In the mid-1990s, I attended several property investment seminars, where seasoned experts shared strategies that opened my eyes to the immense potential of real estate. The advice I received was simple but transformative: During that period, property values often doubled every eight years. Investors were encouraged to leverage equity from existing properties to fund new acquisitions. The idea was to build a portfolio of eight properties, purchasing one each year, and then redraw equity every eight years to fund further investments or personal expenses.

At the time, interest rates were high, hovering around 9 to 10 percent. Despite this, the long-term growth potential outweighed the immediate cost of borrowing. Inspired by this advice, I began to build a portfolio, acquiring six properties in suburbs like Willetton, Ardross, Redcliffe, Balga, and, of course, retaining our property in Canning Vale. Each property came with its unique challenges, but they were all paid for through rental income, making the process manageable.

After successfully building a portfolio, I decided to shift my focus. Rather than continuing to expand, I chose to sell most of my properties to fund the construction of my dream home, the home where I still reside today. The decision was not purely financial: it was about creating a space that reflected our values, aspirations, and the life my wife and I had built together. By this time, only the Canning Vale property remained in my portfolio, serving as a financial anchor.

Finding my dream home

The home I live in today is not just a shelter: it is a manifestation of a dream born from intention, imagination, and unwavering belief. It carries a story that underscores the transformative power of visualising one's aspirations and aligning actions to bring them to life.

My journey to finding this home began after attending a Tony Robbins seminar, where I was inspired to embrace the practice of visualisation with clarity and purpose. Motivated by this newfound perspective, I created a vision poster–a tangible representation of my dreams. At the heart of this poster was my dream home. I imagined every detail: the number of rooms, the colour of the walls, the layout, the position of the carport, and even the kind of light that would stream through the windows. While I was not certain of the specific suburb, I could vividly sense the atmosphere and feel of the space I longed for.

With my vision crystallised, I turned to property magazines, searching for an image that would reflect the home I saw so clearly in my mind. Then, I found it–a photograph of a house that seemed to leap off the page, as if it had been drawn directly from my imagination. This image became the centrepiece of my vision board, a powerful daily reminder of my aspiration and the belief that it could one day become a reality.

This process was not merely about dreaming: it was about combining focus, intention, and purposeful action. I used this vision not as a passive hope but as a guide to align my efforts, decisions, and mindset.

Years later, when I first stepped into what would become my home, I was struck by how closely it mirrored the vision I had crafted years earlier. It was not just similar; it was as though the house had materialised directly from my imagination. This was no coincidence, as it resulted from intentional visualisation and purposeful action.

Finding my dream home has been a profound affirmation of a life lesson: When you dare to dream boldly, visualise with precision, and act with resolve, you can transform the intangible into reality. This house is more than a home: it is a testament to the life-changing potential of clarity, belief, and the boundless possibilities of imagination.

While most of my real estate ventures were profitable, not all investments were successful. One setback occurred in 2013 when I attended a seminar in Perth. The event was endorsed by individuals I held in high regard, lending it an air of credibility. Among the presentations, Rowan Burn from Market First Property Investors promoted an "option plan" investment in Victoria. The pitch was polished, supported by a professional marketing brochure, and seemed like a lucrative opportunity. The proposal involved purchasing two parcels of land through option fees totalling $119,000. A well-known legal firm, Slater and Gordon, handled the contracts, further reinforcing my confidence in the deal.

However, as time passed, cracks began to appear. The developers failed to secure planning approval, and the company eventually went into liquidation. Worse still, the lawyer handling the project was terminated for alleged misconduct. Slater and Gordon, citing conflicts of interest, declined to represent investors like me, leaving us to fend for ourselves. I engaged another legal firm to recover my investment, but the process was slow, costly, and fruitless. The emotional and financial toll was significant, but it taught me a crucial lesson about due diligence, even when dealing with reputable names. Trust, I learned, must always be accompanied by verification.

Another misstep occurred during a holiday in Bali. While exploring the vibrant streets, my wife and I were approached by a street promoter offering an intriguing investment opportunity. The promise was alluring: a holiday home we could own for a set period, with free annual stays and potential rental income. The sales office displayed photographs and letters from prominent Australian figures, including a prime minister, adding an air of legitimacy to the proposal.

Despite my initial hesitancy, I was drawn in by the polished presentation and the hospitable treatment we received. I paid an initial deposit of around $15,000, with my wife by my side, offering her quiet support. However, it did not take long for the cracks to show in that proposal as well. The project required additional management fees, making it financially unviable, and I was forced to accept the loss with no way to recover my deposit.

These experiences taught me that real estate, like life, is a mix of triumphs and setbacks. The profitable ventures reminded me of the potential of calculated risks, while the losses underscored the importance of diligence and caution.

Despite the occasional missteps, most of my real estate ventures were successful. Each property contributed to my financial growth, allowing me to fund my family's needs, pursue my dreams, and eventually build a home that stands as a testament to perseverance and vision. Real estate has been more than an investment for me: it has been a journey of discovery, learning, and growth.

A knighthood

During this time, Andrew was deeply involved with the prestigious Knights of Malta, an ancient and respected organisation with a history dating back centuries. His contributions to medicine and complementary therapies earned him a knighthood from this esteemed order. The title was a mark of his dedication and achievements in advancing healthcare and holistic medicine. At the time, there were very few knights and dames in Perth, making this honour even more exclusive and significant.

Inspired by Andrew's recognition and my own contributions to the field of Natural Therapy Education in Australia, I was nominated for a knighthood by the Knights of Malta. The nomination was a profound acknowledgement of the work we had accomplished in establishing a foundation for complementary medicine education and promoting its value to the broader medical and therapeutic communities.

In 1998, I was officially inducted as a knight in a vestiture ceremony held at the St. Mary's Cathedral in Perth. The event was deeply symbolic and solemn, steeped in tradition and ritual that reflected the legacy of the Knights of Malta. As I knelt before the ceremonial gathering and received my knighthood, I felt an overwhelming sense of pride and gratitude. It was not only a recognition of my efforts but also a testament to the transformative power of education and the tireless work of so many who believed in the future of complementary medicine.

This honour marked a significant milestone in my journey, reinforcing my commitment to the values of service, education, and innovation, which had guided my work in Australia. The title carried with it a sense of responsibility–to continue advancing holistic medicine and to contribute meaningfully to the communities I served. Becoming a Knight of Malta was not only a personal achievement but also a reflection of the growing acceptance of holistic and complementary therapies within broader healthcare practices. At a time when these fields were still finding their footing in Australia, this recognition was a beacon of validation for the work Andrew, myself, and many others were doing to bridge the gap between traditional and alternative medicine.

This honour remains a cherished memory and a reminder of the impact of passion and perseverance in breaking new ground and inspiring others to follow their own paths of innovation and service.

Contributing as president of the Sri Lankan Cultural Society

In 1999, I was honoured to be nominated as the Sri Lankan Cultural Society president in Western Australia. This role brought with it an array of opportunities, challenges, and invaluable lessons. It was both an interesting and demanding position, as it required balancing the diverse expectations of a vibrant community while ensuring the society fulfilled its mission to preserve and promote Sri Lankan culture in Australia.

While serving as president, I faced my share of conflicts and challenges. Differences of opinion arose among members, which occasionally led to misunderstandings and even the loss of a few friendships. Despite these difficulties, I viewed each challenge as an opportunity to grow, learning that leadership demands resilience and the ability to face criticism, no matter how good one's intentions might be. This realisation has stayed with me throughout my life, proving to be a crucial lesson in many of my endeavours.

On the brighter side, my tenure allowed me to forge strong and lasting friendships with many wonderful individuals who shared my passion for the community. These connections enriched my life and opened doors to further involvement in community events and activities.

Among the most precious memories was the chance to serve as a compere or master of ceremonies for several events. Public speaking and hosting were roles I relished, especially when they allowed me to introduce esteemed personalities. One of the highlights was introducing Victor Ratnayake, one of my idols and a legendary Sri Lankan artist, on stage. Standing before a gathering and sharing the same platform with such an iconic figure was a surreal and unforgettable experience.

The year was filled with dynamic events that brought the community together and celebrated our heritage. We organised a New Year's Eve celebration at the Melville Council main hall, complete with a live band, dinner, and dancing. It was a vibrant gathering that showcased the spirit of togetherness within our community.

Among other popular events that we organised was a family trip to Moore River, a delightful escape into the scenic beauty of Western Australia. Families came together to relax, bond, and enjoy the natural surroundings, creating cherished memories.

The young talent show we organised, which showcased the remarkable talents of Sri Lankan youth in Western Australia, became a popular event, celebrating the next generation's creativity and skills. Seeing the pride and enthusiasm of parents and children alike was heartwarming. Another event was the musical evening, a unique and entertaining initiative that invited participants to sing on stage with a live band. Each song carried a $5 donation, turning a night of fun and music into a meaningful fundraising effort. The joy and camaraderie in the room were contagious, making it one of the year's most memorable events.

Reflecting on my time as president, I feel immense gratitude for the opportunity to serve and learn. The role brought a mix of challenges and triumphs but left me with a profound appreciation for the resilience and warmth of our community. I gained invaluable insights into leadership, collaboration, and the art of handling criticism constructively. Most importantly, the experience enriched my personal and professional life, leaving me with countless, joyful memories and a deepened sense of connection to my cultural roots.

After my term as president, I continued to engage with the community in meaningful ways. One particularly enjoyable experience was hosting the Sri Lankan radio program briefly during the regular presenter's absence. This role allowed me to connect with listeners and share news, music, and cultural stories. I embraced this task wholeheartedly, combining my love for communication with my dedication to the Sri Lankan community.

Returning to medicine: a journey of rediscovery

In 2007, amidst the bustling life of running a college, I made the decision to return to my roots in medicine despite maintaining my registration to practice medicine and surgery in Sri Lanka. It was not a decision driven by ambition or career advancement but by a deeply personal desire to update my knowledge and skills in a field that had always been close to my heart. Since leaving Sri Lanka in 1990, I had not actively practised medicine. However, teaching biomedical science to complementary medicine students demanded that I stay current in my knowledge, and I diligently did so by subscribing to medical journals and reading the latest texts. Still, I knew that theoretical knowledge was no substitute for hands-on experience.

Returning to formal medical education after so many years was daunting, requiring commitment, perseverance, and careful planning to balance my college responsibilities with the demands of studying medicine. After extensive research, I found a program that fit my unique circumstances: a medical school in St. Kitts, a beautiful island in the Caribbean.

The university I selected was approved by the Government of St. Kitts and Nevis and accredited by the World Federation for Medical Education (WFME). The MD program offered flexibility in attending lectures and completing clinical placements, making it ideal for someone like me who was already managing a full-time career. The Australian Medical Council validated the degree, ensuring its recognition back home. All these factors gave me the confidence to embark on this challenging journey of returning to practicing medicine.

The application process was rigorous, but I was fortunate to have the support of mentors and colleagues who believed in my vision. Professor Colvin Goonaratne, a faculty member in medical education, provided essential documentation for my application. Dr B.J.C. Perera, a consultant paediatrician under whom I had interned in Badulla, wrote a glowing reference letter, as did Dr U.A. Mendis, the Director General of Health Services in Sri Lanka. Closer to home, Dr. Joseph Thomas, a general practitioner, and Dr. Vivil Dekaw, a general practitioner who had attended my acupuncture classes, added their endorsements.

Reflecting on this period, I realised the profound value of working closely, respectfully, and cooperatively with the people I encountered, especially my superiors. Their help and belief in me were instrumental in securing my admission. These individuals recognised my potential and were willing to vouch for me based on the respect and rapport we had built over the years. This experience reaffirmed my belief in the importance of relationships and the immense difference they can make in one's journey.

The university acknowledged my prior experience by granting substantial credits for the clinical hours I had completed during my internship and medical practice in Sri Lanka. This validation allowed me to continue managing the college while pursuing my medical degree, a delicate balance that required immense discipline and time management.

One of the most enriching aspects of the MD program was the opportunity to complete clinical placements in Australia, which allowed me to bridge the gap between my earlier training and modern medical practices.

At Charles Gairdner Hospital in Perth, I focused on surgical placements, which refreshed my skills and updated me with the latest techniques. Fremantle Hospital offered placements in medicine and surgery, giving me a comprehensive understanding of patient management in different settings. My rotation at the Royal North Shore Hospital in New South Wales concentrated on medicine, while Westmead Hospital provided invaluable experience in paediatrics. At the Royal Prince Alfred Hospital, I gained exposure to gynaecology and obstetrics, a field I found both challenging and fascinating. Finally, at Sentient Private Psychiatric Clinic in Perth, I deepened my understanding of psychiatry, an area of growing importance in modern healthcare.

Each placement brought its own challenges and learning opportunities. Working across various hospitals and specialties allowed me to gain a holistic understanding of medicine while reigniting the passion I had for patient care. These experiences were more than just academic; they were profoundly rewarding on a personal level.

The academic structure of the program was intensive yet stimulating. Unlike traditional semester systems, the curriculum was divided into study blocks. Each block culminated in a time-sensitive online examination supervised by a nominated proctor. My proctor, Mr. Nalin Wijesinghe, an engineer based in Perth, ensured that the examinations were conducted with integrity.

What made the program particularly challenging were the early morning lectures and tutorials delivered live from the United States. Often, I found myself waking up at 2 a.m. to participate, driven by a mix of discipline and passion. The curriculum was modelled on the United States Medical Licensing Examination (USMLE), focusing on integrated clinical studies rather than isolated subjects. This approach made the learning experience engaging and practical.

The faculty members were exceptional, blending academic rigour with real-world insights. My classmates, mostly mature-aged professionals from medical and paramedical backgrounds, added a richness to the learning environment. The shared experiences and camaraderie among us created a supportive and inspiring atmosphere.

Thankfully, all the hard work, sleepless nights, and sacrifices culminated in 2011, when I graduated with my medical degree. The ceremony, held at the prestigious University Club in Chicago, was a moment of immense pride and fulfilment, a testament to my perseverance and the unwavering support of those who had stood by me. My brother-in-law Neminda, who was living in Keppetipola with us and now lived in the United States, attended the ceremony to celebrate this milestone with me. His presence made the day even more unique, reminding me of the family and friendships that had supported me through every step of this journey.

This chapter of my life was more than an academic endeavour; it was a rediscovery of a passion that had been temporarily set aside. Balancing my studies with running the college taught me the value of resilience and the importance of lifelong learning. The experience also deepened my appreciation for the interconnectedness of medicine and education, reinforcing my commitment to making a meaningful impact in both fields.

Most importantly, this journey highlighted the significance of building and maintaining respectful relationships. The help I received from mentors, colleagues, and superiors reminded me that success is rarely a solitary achievement. Often, it is the result of collective effort, where trust, respect, and collaboration pave the way for opportunities to unfold.

Returning to medicine was not just about updating my skills; it was about reaffirming my identity as a medical professional and an educator. The journey was challenging, but the rewards, both personal and professional, were immeasurable. It reminded me that it is never too late to pursue a dream and that with determination, even the most ambitious goals can be achieved.

The rise and fall of VET FEE-HELP and navigating challenges in complementary medicine education

In and around 2009, the Australian Government introduced the VET FEE-HELP (VFH) program, a groundbreaking initiative that provided income-contingent loans to students pursuing higher-level Vocational Education and Training (VET) qualifications. This policy was transformative, enabling access to education for thousands of students who might otherwise have been unable to afford it. Recognising the potential, my college applied to become a provider of VET FEE-HELP-approved courses. To our great satisfaction, our application was successful.

This approval marked a period of exponential growth for the Australian Institute of Holistic Medicine (AIHM). Student numbers increased dramatically, driven by the accessibility of government-backed loans. At the same time, our virtual campus was thriving, allowing us to expand enrolments without physical limitations. We provided intensive clinical training on our Perth campus and offered workplace-based training for those unable to travel. This combination of traditional and innovative education delivery positioned AIHM as a leader in the field at the time.

However, the golden era of VET FEE-HELP was short-lived. By 2015, the Australian Government made sweeping changes to the program, removing many courses from eligibility. Unfortunately, the majority of AIHM's offerings were affected, so the impact on our institution was immediate and profound, with student numbers plummeting overnight.

To compound the issue, in 2013, many associations representing complementary health practitioners announced their intention to only recognise bachelor's degrees in naturopathy and western herbal medicine. This shift excluded the advanced diplomas and diplomas that had long been the backbone of AIHM's curriculum. At the time, I was part of the Industry Consultation Committee for the complementary health profession in Australia. Representing the Australian Council of Private Education and Training, I engaged in intense debates with representatives from various associations. The discussions were often divisive, with some advocating for higher education qualifications while others, like me, pushed for a more inclusive approach that recognised vocational training.

The move to higher education was not just a reflection of industry preferences but also part of a broader shift within complementary medicine education. Since the 1990s, the industry has experienced significant growth, attracting the attention of public universities such as the University of New England, Charles Sturt University, Southern Cross University, the University of Western Sydney, RMIT, and the University of Queensland. These institutions introduced bachelor's degree programs in naturopathy and complementary medicine, which gained popularity.

However, by 2015, most of these programs were discontinued. Mounting pressure from academics and groups critical of complementary medicine led to the growing emphasis on evidence-based medical education. Institutions concerned about maintaining their academic credibility began to withdraw from the field.

Reflecting on this period, I noted a pattern: Concepts and practices that could not be easily measured or validated using conventional scientific tools were often dismissed. Ironically, many such ideas, like the concept of dysbiosis (microbiota imbalance and its impact on health), initially ridiculed by mainstream medicine were later accepted after being validated by emerging research tools. This cycle highlighted the tension between innovation and institutional conservatism.

At this time, only a handful of private education providers continued offering bachelor's degree programs in complementary medicine. One prominent provider operated several campuses across Australia, including Perth, while two others were based in the eastern states. Many of the most vocal advocates for removing advanced diplomas from the national curriculum were associated with these institutions, raising concerns about vested interests. Among professional organisations, only the Australian Traditional Medicine Society advocated for the coexistence of vocational and higher education qualifications, a position I found to be the most sensible.

Recognising the signs of an impending downturn in vocational education, I proposed to my business partner that we transition AIHM into a higher education provider. This required significant financial and organisational investment, but it was essential for our survival. Unfortunately, my business partner did not support the idea. By 2013, our relationship had deteriorated dramatically due to disagreements with multiple business-related matters, which became personal and hurtful, making collaboration increasingly difficult between us. The differences in our vision and approach reached a breaking point, and continuing to work together became impossible.

Given the situation, I proposed buying out my partner's shares in the business. What followed was a period of tense negotiations that required legal involvement. The experience was emotionally draining, but it was necessary to move forward. Eventually, I acquired AIHM's vocational education and training operations while the company's real estate assets were left untouched.

Despite these difficulties, I remained committed to adapting to the changing educational landscape. In 2013, I registered a new business, the Australian Institute of Higher and Further Education (AIHFE), with the aim of becoming a higher education provider. This was a monumental task, requiring the establishment of robust governance and academic structures. To guide the institution, I assembled a governing council chaired by Professor Gabriël Moens, a distinguished academic who won the Australian Award for Law and Legal Studies in 1999 and served as Dean and Professor of Law at Murdoch University at the time. The council included my trusted friends, Professor Tilak Chandratilleke and Associate Professor Lionel Martin, whose wisdom and support were invaluable. I assumed the CEO role, leading the organisation's strategic direction, while the academic board was chaired by Professor Judy Harris, who had previously coordinated the complementary medicine bachelor's program at the University of New England. Other board members included Deepti Shukla, Alex Mora, and my youngest daughter, Kalpana, who generously volunteered their time to help realise this vision.

Preparing for accreditation by the Tertiary Education Quality and Standards Agency (TEQSA) was a rigorous process. It involved developing detailed policies, creating course curricula, securing resources, and ensuring compliance with complex regulatory standards. The preparation took a year, requiring unwavering dedication from everyone involved.

However, as the project progressed, I began to have second thoughts. The scale of the undertaking, combined with the shifting educational landscape, led me to reconsider. After much reflection, I decided to withdraw the TEQSA application. It was a difficult but pragmatic decision, driven by the realisation that continuing with the project might place an unsustainable burden on the organisation.

With the removal of VET FEE-HELP and the exclusion of many popular qualifications from the national training package, AIHM's student numbers declined sharply. By 2018, it became clear that operating on the AIHM campus was no longer feasible. I made the difficult decision to leave the campus and transition to cloud-based delivery, focusing on workplace training for the Advanced Diploma of Ayurveda, the sole qualification that remained viable.

I established a home office in Shelley, smoothly adapting to the new system. While it marked the end of an era for AIHM, it also opened a new chapter filled with opportunities for innovation. This chapter of my journey was one of profound challenges but also resilience and growth. Navigating a deteriorating partnership, adapting to a rapidly changing industry, and making complex decisions tested my resolve in ways I had never imagined. Yet, it also taught me the importance of adaptability, perseverance, and collaboration.

Throughout the journey of building and growing AIHM and AIHFE, many remarkable staff members left their mark. Among them, Kim Ng, our senior administrative secretary, made an extraordinary and lasting contribution. As my right hand, she exemplified unwavering loyalty, dedication, and hard work. Kim stood by me through both triumphs and challenges, embodying steadfast support every step of the way. Her incredible service spanned over 25 years, and she remained with us until the very end of her career, retiring with honour and leaving behind an indelible legacy.

The relationships I built with academic colleagues, trusted friends, and supporters during this time were invaluable. They reminded me that even in the face of adversity, collective effort and shared purpose could lead to new possibilities. Although the journey did not unfold as I had envisioned, it reaffirmed my commitment to education and the belief that challenges often pave the way for growth and innovation.

Studying law and realising a childhood dream of becoming a lawyer

As a young man, I dreamed of becoming a lawyer. My fascination with the profession stemmed from a deep confidence in my communication skills and the thrill I imagined in courtroom advocacy. I pictured myself presenting persuasive arguments, winning cases, and earning recognition for my skills and abilities. Although I did not fully understand the multifaceted role of a lawyer as a young man, the dream persisted, a symbol of ambition and intellectual challenge.

Life, however, had other plans for me. My journey took me down a vastly different path, leading to medicine, business, and education. Yet, as I approached my late fifties, I felt a pull toward that childhood dream of the law. It was not about fame or recognition anymore but about fulfilling a lifelong aspiration and exploring a new frontier of knowledge. With this resolve, I enrolled at the University of New England, located in Armidale in New South Wales, to pursue a Bachelor of Law degree. As that law school offered its degree remotely, it became feasible for me to undertake the studies. As part of my degree program, I even enrolled in a summer program at the University of Ghent, Belgium, where Professor Moens was teaching a course on International Commercial Law for Curtin University.

Embarking on this journey later in life was both exhilarating and demanding. Managing my responsibilities at the college while diving into the intricacies of legal studies required discipline and meticulous time management. I embraced the challenge wholeheartedly, immersing myself in contract law, constitutional law, and the myriad of other subjects that form the backbone of legal education.

In 2018, I achieved what had once seemed like an impossible goal: I graduated with a Bachelor of Laws at the University of New England. It was a moment of immense pride, not only because it represented the fulfilment of a childhood dream but also because it symbolised the power of persistence and lifelong learning.

Although I initially had no intention of practising law, several friends encouraged me to take the next step: admission to the Supreme Court of Western Australia as a lawyer. Their belief in me was infectious, and I decided to pursue this opportunity. To do so, I needed to complete additional requirements, including a graduate diploma in legal practice and a period of supervised legal work.

I enrolled in the College of Law of Western Australia to fulfil the academic component and undertook placements at legal firms in Perth; the experience was both challenging and enlightening. After completing the necessary requirements, I was admitted to the Supreme Court of Western Australia as a lawyer in 2018. It was a proud moment, not only for me but for my family, who had supported me through this transformative journey.

With my admission to the bar, I ventured into legal practice. I began my restrictive practice at a law firm in Perth, which offered flexible work arrangements. Unfortunately, the principal legal practitioner faced health issues that led to the discontinuation of her practice. This sudden change prompted me to explore opportunities with a well-known legal firm in Perth. At this firm, I encountered a vastly different work culture. While the principal was an inspiring mentor, and I learned a great deal in a short time, the rigid expectations of full-time hours were difficult to reconcile with my established commitments and lifestyle. The work culture, though enriching, was not a good fit for me. I decided to resign, but the friendship I built with the principal remains strong to this day, a testament to the value of authentic connections in professional life.

Although I discontinued the practice of law, the skills and knowledge I gained proved invaluable in many aspects of my life, particularly in business. The ability to navigate contracts, understand regulatory frameworks, and think critically through complex issues added a new dimension to my decision-making abilities. Whether in negotiations, compliance, or risk assessment, my legal background became a powerful tool.

The idea that education is never wasted was reinforced in this chapter of my life. Even if a qualification is not used in its traditional sense, the insights and perspectives it offers can enhance one's personal and professional growth in unexpected ways. After stepping away from legal practice, I refocused my energy on the college I built. The timing was serendipitous, as the institution required my full attention during its final years before its sale in 2024. My legal training allowed me to navigate the complexities of the business with confidence, ensuring smooth operations and strategic decision-making.

Studying law and becoming a lawyer was a journey of fulfilment, growth, and self-discovery. It taught me that it is never too late to pursue a dream, no matter how far life takes you in other directions. The process of studying law in my late fifties, managing placements, and achieving admission to the Supreme Court was a testament to the power of resilience and adaptability.

Looking back, I am grateful for the encouragement of friends, the support of mentors, and the opportunities that allowed me to realise this dream. It was not just about becoming a lawyer: it was about proving to myself that age is no barrier to ambition and that every stage of life offers a chance to grow, learn, and achieve something meaningful.

Buying another business: A journey of learning, challenges, and growth

As the demands of managing my college lessened, I found myself restless, yearning for a new adventure. My experience in health and education naturally drew me toward the idea of a childcare business, a venture that seemed like a perfect fit for my background. When I shared this idea with my wife, she, as always, offered her quiet, unwavering support. One of her many remarkable qualities is her belief in my ideas, no matter how ambitious or unconventional they might be. She has been a steadfast partner in my journey, helping when she could, advising when necessary, and trusting me to chart our course together.

I have experienced more wins than losses in my career, but business is never without its pitfalls. I had made a few costly misjudgements in investments, losing around $200,000 in the stock market and property deals. Whenever my wife raised this, I brushed it off with a grin: "Every mistake is a lesson, and this one just came with an expensive tuition fee," I'd say. This philosophy, though cheeky, rang true for me. Life's lessons, whether in business or otherwise, often come at a cost.

Throughout my life, learning has been my unwavering anchor, a compass that has guided me through triumphs and challenges alike. From an early age, I developed a deep-seated belief that to do better, one must first learn and know better. This conviction shaped not just my personal growth but also every decision I made in life and business.

As a teenager, I discovered Dale Carnegie's book, *How to Win Friends and Influence People*, which profoundly impacted me. It was not just a guide to better relationships: it was a blueprint for building a life of financial, spiritual, and social success. That single book unlocked a mindset that encouraged curiosity, reflection, and the pursuit of self-improvement. From that point onward, I sought wisdom from every available source.

Over the years, I immersed myself in the teachings of transformational leaders like Tony Robbins, Zig Ziglar, Jim Rohn, Deepak Chopra, and Ajahn Brahm. Their insights were not just ideas but tools that I applied to reshape my thinking and actions. Whether it was Robbins's strategies for achieving peak performance, Chopra's lessons on mindfulness, or Ajahn Brahm's wisdom on letting go, each perspective enriched my journey.

These mentors, though some I never met in person, became like trusted guides, steering me toward a path of growth and fulfilment.

I have always believed that to rise higher, one must surround themselves with people who excel, those who know better, do better, and inspire better. It is not about envy but admiration and the willingness to learn. I sought the company of successful individuals not just to absorb their knowledge but to adopt their mindsets.

In my businesses, I applied this principle by hiring people who were experts in their fields, trusting their skills to complement my vision. I never felt threatened by their knowledge; instead, I saw their expertise as an opportunity to elevate our collective efforts. The humility to recognise my own limitations and the willingness to learn from others became cornerstones of my leadership.

I shared these beliefs with my students, urging them to seek mentors and emulate the paths of those they admired. I often reminded them, "You do not have to reinvent the wheel. Someone has done it before, and probably better. Learn from them." My message was always clear: success does not come from trying to do it all alone; it comes from standing on the shoulders of those who came before us.

Gratitude has been another pillar of my values, as I deeply appreciate the people who have supported me along the way: my family, friends, employees, and mentors. Their contributions have been integral to my successes, and I have made it a priority to acknowledge their efforts.

For instance, during some of the most challenging periods in my career, it was the steadfast support of my wife that kept me grounded. Her willingness to embrace my ideas, even when they seemed risky, gave me the courage to move forward. Similarly, friends like Minoka, who offered kindness and encouragement during trying times, reminded me of the strength found in nurturing connections with people.

I have always believed that the key to a fulfilling life is not just achieving success but recognising and appreciating those who help you get there. Whether it is a small gesture or a monumental act of support, I make it a point to express gratitude to others.

At the heart of my philosophy is the belief that success is far more about attitude than aptitude. Knowledge and skills are essential, but they are amplified by the right mindset; I have seen this repeatedly in my own life and in the lives of my students. The willingness to embrace challenges, adapt to change, and maintain a positive outlook has been a defining factor in my journey.

This mindset is something I have passed on to others as well, encouraging them to pursue their passions with confidence and resilience. I would tell my students, "Act like an expert, and you will become one. Confidence is the bridge between potential and achievement."

Learning, surrounding myself with excellence, expressing gratitude, and maintaining a growth-oriented mindset have been the principles that shaped my decisions and defined my life. They are not just values I hold; they are the essence of who I am. These beliefs have taught me that life is not about perfection but progress, and for that, I remain eternally grateful.

Back to the start of this section, In 2018, I took my first step into the childcare industry, purchasing a small centre in Gingin, a charming town seventy-five minutes from my home. My goal was twofold: Provide workplace training for my students while expanding into childcare qualifications. The owner was going through a family separation and listed the business at $85,000. Feeling empathetic, I decided not to negotiate and offered her the full price.

This was my first time acquiring an established business, as I had always built businesses from scratch, so this was a steep learning curve. Staffing was my first major challenge. The team of fewer than ten employees was unlike any group I had managed before. Gossip, bickering, and resistance to change plagued the workplace. The financial strain was exacerbated by the centre's small enrolment numbers and an unreasonably high lease.

My weekly visits became gruelling, as I spent hours shuttling supplies from Perth and mediating staff issues. Over time, the spark I once felt for the business dimmed, and after a year and a half, the difficulties outweighed any joy I had hoped to find in the venture.

During the particularly challenging times of running the childcare centre, my son, Chaturanga, and daughter-in-law, Nhung, stepped in to support me in ways that made a real difference. The struggles of managing the centre, staff conflicts, high operational costs, and my own lack of experience in the childcare industry were taking a toll on me. Their brief involvement brought a much-needed sense of relief and stability at times.

Then came COVID-19, which devastated all my businesses. The childcare centre endured the most of it, with children staying home and revenues plummeting. Government support packages offered a lifeline, and my staff urged me to keep the business afloat. But by 2021, I knew it was time to let go, so I sold the business at a loss and walked away with an immense sense of relief. This chapter of my life, though challenging, was a testament to resilience and the power of learning through experience. As I closed the book on the childcare business, I felt a renewed sense of purpose and a commitment to focus on what truly mattered to me.

Reflecting on my experience with the childcare centre, there are several things I would approach differently if I were to buy another childcare business. These lessons, though hard-earned, provide valuable insights into navigating such ventures. One of my biggest missteps was purchasing the business without negotiating or deeply analysing its financial and operational details. While my empathy for the seller's personal situation influenced my decision, I now realise the importance of conducting a thorough investigation into the business's performance, enrolment trends, and overall profitability before committing to a purchase.

The staffing challenges were significant hurdles. I underestimated how crucial it is to have a team whose values align with my own and who are adaptable to new leadership styles. If I were to do this venture again, I would spend more time assessing the team dynamics and ensuring proper onboarding and training to establish mutual trust and respect.

The small size of the town and limited population in Gingin posed challenges for maintaining consistent enrolment. If I were to buy a childcare business now, I would focus on a location with a higher demand for childcare services and a more stable population to ensure a steady stream of revenue. Also, the high lease for the centre significantly impacted its profitability. A critical lesson is to negotiate favourable lease terms or ensure the rent aligns with the expected revenue potential of the business.

My weekly visits, though well-intentioned, were insufficient to address the deeper issues within the team and operations. If I were to manage another centre, I would ensure a more consistent and hands-on presence, especially during the initial months, to build a cohesive team and address challenges promptly.

Childcare was an industry in which I had limited expertise, so I would have sought mentors or consultants with deep knowledge of the childcare sector to guide my decisions and help me avoid common pitfalls. It is said that with the benefit of hindsight, every person would be wiser. While my journey with the childcare business was fraught with challenges, it provided invaluable lessons that will shape my approach to future ventures. Had I applied these insights earlier, the outcome might have been different. But as always, every stumble is an opportunity to grow, and for that, I remain grateful.

Additional challenges

The challenges at AIHFE, a Registered Training Organisation (RTO), were different but no less daunting. Workshops and clinical training were disrupted by lockdowns, leaving students frustrated; vaccine hesitancy among some students added another layer of complexity. To adapt, I purchased a dedicated training facility and clinic in Medina, giving me greater control over our operations.

We operated the student clinic in Medina for a brief period, but recurring staff challenges and conflicts forced me to temporarily close it until I could find a suitable practitioner to oversee its operations.

After failing to find a qualified candidate locally, I expanded my search globally by advertising the position internationally. A few applicants responded, and I interviewed one from India who had both academic and clinical experience. After careful consideration, I decided to sponsor her under the employer-sponsored visa category.

The sponsorship was approved, and I enrolled her in a training program to enhance her qualifications, enabling her to deliver effective training and assess Australian students. However, the practitioner later informed me that she had been involved in a serious motor vehicle accident in India, raising doubts about her ability to arrive or commence work as scheduled.

Although this situation caused me to question my decision, I chose to honour my commitment and left the final decision to the candidate. She assured me that her mobility issues were temporary and expected to resolve them within a few months. Additionally, she shared her long-held aspiration to migrate to Australia with her new husband. Believing this opportunity would support her dream of becoming an Australian citizen, I decided to keep the sponsorship open.

Once her arrival was confirmed, I began searching for suitable accommodations. Given the difficulty of securing a rental lease at the time, I decided to purchase a two-bedroom apartment in Medina and offered it to her at a 50 percent discounted rental rate. My wife and I personally picked her up from the airport and welcomed her into our home until she adjusted to the area and the country. After a few days, we helped her move into her new apartment.

A few weeks after her arrival, we organised an intensive clinical workshop for our final-year students. To ensure the clinic's smooth functioning, we brought in an experienced senior practitioner to manage operations, with the new practitioner assisting until she became familiar with the system. The workshop attracted several students, including participants from eastern states and two from overseas.

On the second day of the workshop, I fell ill and tested positive for COVID-19. This was my first encounter with the virus, and it severely affected my health, preventing me from visiting the Medina clinic for several days. During my absence, the senior practitioner and the new practitioner managed the clinic, while I provided guidance and assistance remotely.

The Medina chapter turned into a whirlwind of challenges that I could not have imagined. In the middle of an intensive clinical workshop for final-year students, Roopa Rao, our senior practitioner, called with troubling news. "Some students are complaining of itchy rashes," she said. Assuming it was a mild allergy or irritation, I advised her to monitor the situation.

The next day, the calls turned urgent. "One of the students found ticks," Roopa said. My stomach dropped. Ticks in the clinic? In my three decades of running educational facilities, I had never encountered anything like this. Pest controllers were called in immediately to fumigate the space, and we assumed the problem was resolved. But on the third day, I received another frantic call: The rashes had spread, and tensions were boiling over. The students were furious, demanding answers and accusing me of negligence. For the first time in my career, I found myself on the defensive, facing angry students who were not shy about voicing their frustrations.

With the clinic unusable, I scrambled to secure an alternative venue. The City of Kwinana offered Medina Hall across the road; it was an empty shell, and we had less than twenty-four hours to transform it into a functioning clinic. One evening during this chaotic period, as exhaustion threatened to overwhelm us, my brother Chaminda and our dear friend Minoka became unexpected heroes. Chaminda, always dependable, worked tirelessly alongside me to finalise the setup. A few other friends and family members came to help also.

Meanwhile, after a few hours of helping her daughter set up the cubicles, Minoka made a simple but heartfelt offer. "You all look like you've been through a war," she said gently. "Come to my place for dinner when you're done."

That evening, as we sat at Minoka's dining table, savouring the meal she had lovingly prepared, we found solace in her kindness. It was not just food; it was an act of compassion that reminded us of the strength of community. After dinner, my brother, Chaminda and I returned to the hall, working late into the night to ensure the makeshift clinic was ready for the next day. By midnight, the transformation was complete. It was not perfect, but it was functional, and in those circumstances, this was more than enough.

Sadly, it quickly became apparent that Medina Hall was far from ideal for our needs. The constant assembly and disassembly of clinic cubicles strained resources and morale. I felt as though I was hitting a brick wall. For the second time, I broke down and cried uncontrollably, overcome by helplessness. I could not shake the feeling that I had let the students down, even though it was not due to any negligence on my part. The students had great hopes for a smooth and supportive training environment, and I had worked hard to provide that for them. Once again, my wife was there to console me.

The practitioner I sponsored from India to manage the clinic changed her behaviour within a few weeks. She aligned herself with some of the more radical and difficult students in voicing her opinion while continuing to live in the apartment I had offered her at a 50 percent discount and work in my organisation as an employee. Her actions made everything much more difficult for me, and I struggled to believe how quickly things deteriorated.

Frustrated but determined, I boldly decided to convert my residence into a makeshift clinic. Fortunately, my wife, ever the pillar of support, came on board without hesitation. Together, we transformed our home into a fully operational clinic. My daughter-in-law, Nhung, came with her co-workers and helped us set it up. All the bedrooms were converted into consultation rooms, while the formal living area became a tutorial and case discussion space. It was a heroic effort, but the students could finally continue their training. We cancelled the regular clients who had bookings for the Medina clinic, inviting all our friends and known people for Ayurveda consultation and treatment and offering them the services free of charge.

To ease the students' tensions and frustrations, my wife went above and beyond, preparing home-cooked meals for all of them every single day for the remaining ten days of the clinic. Her generosity and care created a sense of warmth and community, even in the most trying circumstances.

I requested an immediate meeting with the practitioner I sponsored from India following the workshop to discuss the issues. However, she avoided my attempts to meet face to face with her to discuss her concerns and failed to attend the proposed meeting. Considering the considerable trouble she had caused in such a short period, I suspected she lacked the courage to face me. Instead, she sent an email stating she was unable to attend. Given the circumstances, I had no other option but to issue her a letter of termination and notify the Department of Immigration. Later, I learned that she had vacated my apartment and moved in with a friend.

With all these unprecedented events, I felt a clear and undeniable urge to stop what I was doing. There was no encouragement to continue; instead, I found myself surrounded by obstacles at every turn.

During my education career, while owning and managing two educational institutions, I made it a priority to celebrate the success of our students with an annual graduation ceremony. These events were designed to emulate university graduations, complete with formal regalia for both graduates and teachers, followed by a celebratory dinner. The teachers participated in a graduation march as part of the ceremony.

As a personal initiative, I also recognised community leaders at each graduation, presenting them with trophies or medals to honour their contributions. These events were well-supported by industry professional bodies and various companies in Australia that specialised in nutritional and natural therapy products. These organisations generously provided gifts and certificates of recognition to graduates who excelled in their studies, commitment, and service.

Over the years, we held twenty-eight graduation ceremonies across multiple locations in Western Australia, with the final one taking place in January 2024. Determined to make this last ceremony truly special, I not only celebrated the graduates but also presented awards to several teachers and community leaders who had made significant contributions to the industry and humanity.

This final ceremony was a heartfelt celebration that included family and friends. My youngest daughter, Kalpana, served as the MC and performed an inspirational song for the graduates. My elder daughter, Poornima, and her husband, Todd, captivated the audience with a romantic Latin dance they choreographed at my request. Our dear friend Deepti performed a beautiful Indian dance, while another close friend, Praneeth, managed the sound for the evening. Kaushalya, a trusted friend, captured the event's special moments with his photography. To add a unique touch, a professional belly dancer brought energy and excitement to the night.

It was a bittersweet occasion, marking the culmination of my thirty-four-year career in education and my stewardship of these two institutions, a mixture of sadness and pride as I reflected on the many lives touched and the legacy created through these celebrations.

Despite the efforts and sacrifices, the challenges eventually took their toll. By February 2024, it was clear that my passion for running the business had waned. A chance encounter at a seminar led to a buyer, and after careful negotiations, I sold the business.

Some students expressed disappointment, but I made every effort to ensure their smooth transition, arranging for credits to transfer to another provider. The sale marked the close of a tumultuous chapter in my life and career but also opened the door to new possibilities.

Through the difficulties, one truth remained clear: The unwavering support of my family and friends carried me through. Chaminda's steadfastness, Minoka's generosity, and my wife's enduring patience reminded me that even in the darkest times, the strength of those around us can light the way forward.

Life is a series of chapters, each with its own trials and triumphs. As I prepared to embark on my next journey, I carried with me the wisdom gained from this experience and a determination to keep growing, learning, and contributing.

CHAPTER 7
Navigating Health Concerns

After selling my educational establishment, I experienced a profound sense of relief, as it felt like I had finally unburdened myself from years of relentless work and challenges. I was eager to take a well-deserved break; yet, the idea of doing "nothing" did not sit well with me. Retirement was not a word I associated with my life. To me, retirement symbolised stagnation, a metaphorical, invalid stamp, and I was determined not to let that define me.

I envisioned the remaining part of my life as an opportunity to do something meaningful. Though I was sixty-seven, my mindset and ambitions aligned more with someone in their twenties. I felt energetic, both physically and mentally, and was ready to channel that energy into new pursuits.

For over a decade, I had maintained an active lifestyle. I cycled about 24 kilometres 3 to 4 times a week and, on days I did not ride, I walked approximately 8 kilometres. If the weather was unsuitable for outdoor activity, I kept myself fit by riding a stationary exercise bike at home. I often told myself that since I taught wellness, I needed to live it, too; I wanted to "walk my talk."

My diet was healthy, though I allowed myself occasional indulgences. I enjoyed chocolates and sweets now and then, along with a glass or two of red wine, especially in good company. Life, I believed, should be about balance–nourishing the body and the soul while leaving room for simple pleasures.

Having spent decades immersed in professional life, I yearned to explore my spiritual side and rediscover the artistic talents I had left dormant. The teachings of the Buddha resonated deeply with me. However, I also respected all religions and appreciated their value, if they promoted harmony and avoided harm.

I began intensifying my Buddhist practices, listening to Dhamma talks online and revisited books that had profoundly influenced me, such as *The Power of Now: A Guide to Spiritual Enlightenment* by Eckhart Tolle. Ajahn Brahm's sermons and teachings by other monks and lay practitioners offered me new perspectives. Meditation became a regular part of my daily routine, helping me connect with my inner self.

I also spent some time learning to play my Yamaha keyboard and thoroughly enjoyed singing along, allowing myself to dream freely. Manju, a fellow Sri Lankan, taught me the basics of playing the keyboard. He was also kind enough to give me the opportunity to showcase my keyboard and singing skills at one of his concerts in Perth.

For years, I had wanted to author a book, an autobiography detailing my journey and sharing the lessons I had learned along the way. I envisioned creating a personal website to offer coaching and mentoring, sharing my experiences through a YouTube channel. Additionally, I wanted to engage in voluntary work, giving back to the community that had given me so much.

These ideas swirled in my mind, but I decided not to rush into anything. For at least six months, I planned to focus on myself, taking a step back to recalibrate and enjoy the freedom I had earned. In the meantime, I immersed myself in a small construction project at home–a studio apartment that I had been planning for some time. Cycling remained a vital part of my routine, helping me stay grounded and energised.

Physically, I felt fit, though I was mindful of a few underlying health issues. My blood pressure and blood sugar levels were borderline, but I managed them through regular check-ups with my GP. Despite these precautions, I noticed troubling symptoms, such as shortness of breath (dyspnoea) during cycling and walking, which progressively worsened. Some days, climbing the stairs at home felt daunting.

I shared these concerns with my GP and cardiologist, who initially did not consider them alarming. Together, we adopted a proactive but non-urgent approach, making decisions collaboratively.

At one point, my GP suggested a coronary calcium score test to assess my heart health. This test measures calcium deposits in the coronary arteries, which supply blood to the heart. Over time, calcium can accumulate in the arteries, contributing to plaque formation and narrowing the vessels–a condition known as atherosclerosis. The calcium score serves as an indicator of the risk for coronary artery disease (CAD).

The procedure was non-invasive: A CT scan captured detailed images of my heart, and the calcium deposits were quantified. Unfortunately, my calcium score returned quite high (634), indicating significant plaque buildup. This was concerning, as it suggested an elevated risk for coronary artery disease. However, both my GP and cardiologist believed my active lifestyle and current mild medication regimen were sufficient at that stage, reassuring me that urgent intervention was not necessary.

Another concern was a mild elevation in my cholesterol and triglyceride levels. While these findings could not warrant the use of statins, widely prescribed anti-cholesterol drugs, my cardiologist and I agreed to explore alternatives and introduce a small dose of statin. He also recommended a regimen of nutritional supplements supported by emerging evidence:

Vitamin K2: This vitamin plays a crucial role in directing calcium in the body. It ensures that calcium is deposited in bones and teeth, where it belongs, rather than accumulating in the arteries as plaque. Vitamin K2 also works synergistically with Vitamin D to enhance calcium metabolism and support cardiovascular health.

Ubiquinol: This is the active, antioxidant form of Coenzyme Q10 (CoQ10), essential for energy production in cells. It is particularly important for heart health, as the heart requires a constant supply of energy. Ubiquinol also has antioxidant properties, helping to reduce oxidative stress, which is a contributing factor in atherosclerosis.

Bergamot (Bergomet): Derived from bergamot oranges, this supplement contains polyphenols that can help lower cholesterol levels and improve lipid profiles. Bergamot has been shown to reduce LDL cholesterol ("bad cholesterol") and triglycerides while increasing HDL cholesterol ("good cholesterol"). Its anti-inflammatory and antioxidant effects also support overall cardiovascular health.

To further investigate my symptoms, my GP arranged an exercise echocardiogram, also known as a stress echocardiogram. This test evaluates how the heart performs under physical stress. Initially, I underwent a resting echocardiogram, where an ultrasound captured images of my heart's chambers, valves, and blood flow. Then, I exercised on a treadmill, gradually increasing intensity while technicians monitored my heart's response.

The results were encouraging; there was no evidence of myocardial ischemia, meaning my heart muscles were receiving sufficient blood flow even under stress. However, the test revealed features of apical hypertrophic cardiomyopathy (HCM), a condition where the heart muscle at the apex becomes abnormally thickened, potentially affecting its function.

Hypertrophic cardiomyopathy is often inherited, though its exact cause is not always known. In some cases, it may result from long-standing high blood pressure or other factors. The thickened heart muscle can make it harder for the heart to pump blood efficiently. Fortunately, my case was mild and did not require immediate intervention, so my GP and cardiologist decided to monitor it closely with my consent.

One persistent issue I faced was insomnia. Since falling out with my business partner, I struggled to stay asleep through the night. I had no trouble falling asleep initially, but I would wake around 2 a.m. and often could not return to sleep. I tried various techniques, including meditation and lifestyle adjustments, but the problem persisted. It became a subtle yet constant reminder of the emotional toll of past conflicts.

Despite these health challenges, I remained optimistic. Life had taught me resilience, and I was determined to keep moving forward, embracing every opportunity to grow, learn, and contribute. As I embarked on this new phase, I saw it as a continuation of my journey, a chapter filled with possibilities where I could explore new dimensions of life and share my experiences with others. The next phase of my life beckoned, full of lessons to be learned, new experiences to embrace, and opportunities to make a difference. Little did I know how much more this journey had in store for me.

Health scare

One evening in April 2024, I set out for my usual 24-kilometre bike ride. The air was cool, and the roads were quiet, a perfect setting for reflection and physical exercise. However, this ride was unlike any other.

About eight kilometres into the journey, I began to feel an unsettling tightness in my chest, just between my shoulder blades. Breathing became increasingly difficult, and a dull discomfort spread to my upper abdomen.

I stopped riding and rested on a bench by the side of the road, but I did not feel a significant relief. I could not ignore the possibility that these symptoms might be a warning sign of angina, a prelude to a heart attack, or even a mild heart attack itself. However, a part of me wanted to downplay the severity, convincing myself it was just muscle pain. Determined not to alarm my wife, who would undoubtedly panic, I decided to ride home slowly, stopping frequently to catch my breath.

Eventually, I reached home and went straight to my room, feeling drained and uneasy. I told my wife I was not feeling well and needed rest. With my response, I noticed some signs of anxiety on her face. I naively decided to wait until the next day to see my GP–a mistake many of us make in critical moments. Thankfully, my youngest daughter, Kalpana, was at home. She insisted I go to the hospital immediately and drove me to Fiona Stanley Hospital (FSH), with my wife accompanying us.

At the emergency department, I described my symptoms and history. The admission nurse took my concerns seriously, and I was admitted immediately. After a brief wait, I was taken to a ward where an electrocardiogram (ECG) was performed. The emergency physician informed me that while the ECG showed some irregularities, it was not definitive for a heart attack. To confirm, they ordered a blood test to check for cardiac enzymes.

Cardiac enzymes, such as troponin, are proteins released into the bloodstream when the heart muscle is damaged, such as during a heart attack. Elevated levels of these enzymes are a key indicator of cardiac events. A few hours later, the results were in: my cardiac enzymes were significantly elevated, confirming I had suffered a myocardial infarction (heart attack).

That night, I was confined to bed and scheduled for an emergency coronary angiogram to determine the extent of the damage. A coronary angiogram is a diagnostic procedure that uses X-ray imaging to examine the blood vessels of the heart. A thin catheter is inserted into a blood vessel, usually in the groin or wrist, and guided to the coronary arteries. A contrast dye is injected, allowing doctors to see blockages or narrowing in the arteries.

The angiogram revealed a sobering reality: all three of my coronary arteries were significantly blocked beyond what could be addressed with angioplasty. In angioplasty, a small balloon is inflated inside the blocked artery to open it, often accompanied by the placement of a stent to keep it open. My condition, however, required a more invasive intervention: coronary artery bypass grafting (CABG).

The next morning, Dr. Felicity Lee, my cardiologist, visited me with her team of registrars. Her bubbly, friendly demeanour instantly put me at ease despite the gravity of the situation. We discussed my options, and she explained that CABG was the best course of action. CABG involves creating new pathways for blood to flow to the heart by grafting arteries or veins from other parts of the body. Dr. Lee recommended one of the top cardiothoracic surgeons, Dr. Rob Larbalestier, who specialised in off-pump CABG, a technique performed while the heart is still beating, avoiding the use of a heart-lung machine.

Off-pump CABG has several advantages, including reduced bleeding, a lower risk of complications such as stroke, and shorter recovery times. Dr. Larbalestier also used both arteries and vein grafts. Arterial grafts have greater longevity and are less likely to develop blockages compared to vein grafts.

I trusted Dr. Lee's judgment and agreed to transfer to a private hospital where Dr. Larbalestier performed surgeries. Two days after my admission to the private hospital, I underwent coronary artery bypass grafting (CABG), a life-saving surgical procedure to restore blood flow to my heart. I was fortunate to have private insurance, which covered the entire procedure and hospital stay, alleviating financial stress during this critical time.

Dr. Larbalestier and his skilled surgical team performed complex operations with precision and care. The surgery lasted 4 to 5 hours. During the procedure, they used a combination of grafts: a radial artery from my arm, a saphenous vein from my leg, and an internal mammary artery from my chest. These grafts were carefully selected and meticulously connected to bypass the blocked coronary arteries, creating new pathways for blood to reach my heart muscle.

This experience highlighted not only the importance of skilled medical care and comprehensive health coverage but also the incredible advancements in cardiac surgery that save countless lives each year. It serves as a reminder of the resilience of the human body and the extraordinary efforts of medical professionals to give patients a second chance at life.

On the first night after my surgery, I was met with an unexpected and challenging experience at the private hospital. The room, designed for two patients, was less than ideal for anyone seeking rest and recovery. Sharing the space with another patient, I quickly realised the strain this setup placed on both of us. Privacy was scarce, and shared amenities like the bathroom became a source of inconvenience. The comings and goings of visitors added to the chaos, further disturbing the fragile peace we sought during our recovery.

When I needed assistance from a nurse, her dismissive response left me feeling isolated and neglected. Later that night, the ringing of the call bell brought no help, amplifying my sense of vulnerability. The following day, I mustered the courage to file a formal complaint against the hospital. The hospital management later admitted that the call bell system had malfunctioned and assured me they had since rectified the issue. By a twist of fate, my situation improved significantly when the other patient was discharged, allowing me the privacy and comfort of a single room.

Fearing to what had happened on the first night, my family and I requested to allow one of our own carers to stay at night The hospital authorities initially did not want to oblige our request, so we had to persuade them to allow us to have someone at night sit with me due to my experience of the previous night, and reluctantly, they agreed. When all the negotiations took place at the hospital, our trusted family friends Rajesh and Deepti visited to see me. Rajesh, with his characteristic kindness, offered to stay with me throughout the night, despite my brother's willingness to do so. This act of selflessness was deeply moving. Rajesh and Deepti became more than friends during this challenging time; they became family. Their unwavering support reminded me of the extraordinary bond that genuine concern and empathy can forge.

My family rallied around me with unwavering commitment. My three children visited daily, their presence a balm for my spirit. My elder daughter, bringing along my grandchildren, filled the room with laughter and joy, offering a welcome distraction from the stark reality of my situation. My brother's daily visits and the warmth of friends who came by to express their concerns infused me with strength and hope. My daughter-in-law brought some homemade Vietnamese soup made by her sisters to make me feel better and stimulate my appetite. The hospital staff and doctors, despite initial lapses, contributed to my recovery, demonstrating that collective effort and kindness are powerful healers.

The surgery was successful, though I developed minor atrial fibrillation (AF) afterwards. AF is an irregular heart rhythm that can cause palpitations, fatigue, and other symptoms. To address this, my cardiologist attempted cardioversion, a procedure that uses electrical shocks to restore normal heart rhythm. Unfortunately, it did not work, so I was started on a medication called amiodarone, a strong rhythm-controlling drug. While effective, amiodarone has significant side effects, so the dosage should be tapered carefully.

A few days after being discharged, I experienced a frightening episode. While showering, I suddenly began sweating profusely, felt dizzy, and became nauseous. Kalpana, who came to check on me, noticed my sudden change. As I struggled to stay conscious, she held me up and yelled to her mother to call an ambulance.

The paramedics arrived and performed an ECG, which initially did not show abnormalities. However, subsequent readings revealed significant changes, and they decided to transport me to the hospital. Navigating the narrow staircase in my home to get me to the ambulance was a challenge, but they managed.

At the hospital, it was determined that my atrial fibrillation had worsened due to the premature reduction of amiodarone. I was readmitted and monitored for several days before being discharged with a more gradual medication tapering plan.

At the request of my surgeon, I was transferred from Fiona Stanley Hospital to Mount Hospital, where the cardiac team who performed the surgery monitored my heart for any signs of closure. Reluctantly, I agreed to go to Mount Hospital again, as I felt very homely and comfortable with the FSH. I spent approximately four days in the hospital under close observation before being discharged. Once home, my living arrangements were adjusted for better accessibility, with my room moved to a ground-floor location to prepare for any potential emergencies or complications. Both my wife and Kalpana took on the role of vigilant caregivers, diligently monitoring my condition and supporting me with daily walks and breathing exercises to aid my recovery.

Through this ordeal, I was deeply grateful for the expertise and care of Dr. Felicity Lee, Dr. Rob Larbalestier, and the entire medical team. Their skill and dedication were instrumental in my recovery. Humour and positivity also played roles in keeping my spirits high. This experience reinforced the importance of proactive health management, listening to one's body, and trusting medical professionals. It also reminded me of the fragility of life and the importance of cherishing every moment. As I moved forward, I was more determined than ever to embrace life fully and share the lessons I had learned. The next chapter of my life awaited, filled with new possibilities and the promise of making every moment count.

New lifestyle changes

Upon returning home, the outpouring of love from my community continued. My Sri Lankan friends brought homemade delicacies, easing the burden on my wife, who had already been carrying so much on her shoulders. These small yet meaningful gestures spoke volumes about the strength of community and the enduring power of compassion.

Determined to regain my health, I adhered rigorously to the prescribed exercises and walking routine. My wife, ever vigilant, stood by me, ensuring my safety and encouraging me at every step. Occasionally, my children joined me, turning what could have been a solitary exercise into moments of connection and joy.

This period of recovery became a time of introspection. The scars left by surgery were not merely physical reminders but symbols of resilience and the journey I had undertaken. Though I had hoped to attend my nephew's wedding in Sri Lanka, my wife's wise counsel prevailed, and I reluctantly cancelled the trip. It was a decision made with great difficulty, but it underscored the importance of patience and prioritising health.

Looking back, this experience was a powerful teacher. I learned the importance of speaking up when something is amiss, as I did with the hospital's call bell system. It taught me the value of community and how the love and support of family and friends are instrumental in healing. Most importantly, it reminded me of the resilience of the human spirit. Recovery is not just about physical healing: it is a testament to the strength derived from the people who stand by you and the courage to embrace each day with gratitude and determination.

One of the most profound lessons I have learned from my health journey is the non-typical nature of a heart attack and how it can manifest in unexpected ways. Contrary to the textbook descriptions I studied in medical school, my experience did not fit the classic symptoms often outlined in medical literature.

Instead of the textbook signs, I had trouble breathing, an unsettling symptom that, at the time, did not immediately signal a cardiac event to me. In hindsight, I realise how crucial it would have been to insist on further investigation, including an angiogram. This diagnostic tool could have revealed blockages in my coronary arteries, allowing for early intervention with a stent. Such a proactive approach might have prevented the need for coronary bypass surgery altogether.

This experience taught me a lesson I feel compelled to share with others: heart attacks do not always follow a predictable script. Awareness of non-typical symptoms, like unexplained breathlessness, can make all the difference. Early detection and intervention can save lives and spare individuals from more invasive procedures.

By sharing this, I hope to inspire others to advocate for their health and seek comprehensive evaluations when something feels amiss. It is a reminder that listening to your body and acting promptly can change the course of your health journey.

This time in my life is more than a narrative of illness and recovery: it is a celebration of relationships, resilience, and the enduring power of human kindness. Let it serve as a reminder that even in our darkest hours, light can be found in the love of those around us and in the courage to move forward.

New path

After dedicating forty-four years to a diverse and fulfilling career in medicine, education, health and wellness, law, and business, I have chosen to embark on a new chapter in my life. This chapter is about giving back to the community in a profoundly meaningful way by sharing my life journey, experiences, accumulated knowledge, and the invaluable lessons I have learned along the way. Through this endeavour, I hope to inspire, educate, and empower others, leaving a legacy that reflects the richness of my experiences and the wisdom they have brought me.

As I began to regain my health and embrace life anew, I revisited the plans that had been momentarily sidelined by my cardiac episode. This time, they carried a renewed sense of urgency and purpose. One of my first endeavours was to create a personal website, www.sarathjayawardana.com, which now serves as a platform to share my journey, insights, and aspirations with a broader audience. This digital space is more than just a website: it is a testament to resilience, growth, and the unyielding human spirit.

I joined St John's Ambulance Australia and the Red Cross to do some voluntary work. These organisations have provided me with the opportunity to give back to the community in meaningful ways, turning my challenges into stepping-stones for service. Such work has added a profound layer of fulfilment to my life, showing me the joy of making even a small difference in someone else's journey.

I intend to establish my podcast channel, a creative outlet where I share experiences, lessons, and practical advice. This platform is another way for me to engage with a global audience, spreading positivity and hope. In the next chapter, I will be sharing various lessons I learnt from my life's endeavours, my values and belief that made me who I am today and hope that the information and experiences expressed make a significant difference in the life of my readers.

Looking forward, my plans are bold and brimming with purpose. I intend to continue coaching and mentoring individuals, leveraging the extensive knowledge, skills, and experiences I have gathered through my personal and professional life. Whether through one-on-one guidance, writing, or public speaking, my aim remains steadfast: To empower others to overcome their own obstacles and achieve their dreams.

I aspire to author more books, each one delving deeper into the myriad facets of life, offering insights and lessons that can resonate universally. My vision extends to public speaking, where I can connect with audiences directly, sharing stories that inspire action and change. At the same time, I am committed to exploring my hobbies and nurturing my spiritual awakening, balancing the practical with the profound.

Health and well-being have become a top priority in this chapter of my life. I have embraced a proactive approach to maintaining both physical and mental fitness, and it has become an integral part of my daily routine. My current focus lies in combining structured exercise with mindful habits to support a healthier, more balanced lifestyle so that I can continue to do what I love doing and not become a burden to the community or my loved ones.

After thoughtful consideration, I decided to take my fitness regimen to the next level by joining a gym. While I have always valued walking and cycling, I realised the importance of diversifying my workouts to address both cardiovascular health and muscle strength. With a gym membership in hand, I committed to a routine that includes a mix of cardio- and strength-training exercises.

I now dedicate approximately 1 to 2 hours each day to my workouts. These sessions are carefully structured to include activities that elevate my heart rate, such as treadmill running or cycling, alongside resistance training and weightlifting exercises to build and maintain muscle mass. This balance has not only improved my stamina and strength but has also enhanced my mood, focus, and overall sense of well-being.

As I draw this chapter of my life to a close, I find myself reflecting on the profound lessons that have shaped my journey: the trials that tested me, the triumphs that lifted me, and the values that have been my compass. Each decision I made, each path I walked, was guided by a steadfast belief in the power of the human mind and body, the importance of embracing holistic wellness, and the transformative impact of lifelong learning. These experiences have instilled in me an unwavering commitment to share the insights I have gathered to empower others to live fuller, healthier, and more meaningful lives.

CHAPTER 8
What Made Me Who I Am?

Our lives are a tapestry woven from the threads of values, beliefs, and actions. These are the core principles that define who we are, and while they are influenced by the world around us—the people we meet, the books we read, and the experiences we live through—they remain within our control. Understanding this truth has been the cornerstone of my journey.

From an early age, I recognised the power of association. I was deliberate about the friends I chose and the people I surrounded myself with. This was not a matter of exclusivity but of alignment, seeking out those who shared or inspired the values I wished to cultivate. By spending time with individuals who challenged and motivated me, I was constantly encouraged to strive for better.

This conscious decision was not always easy, as there were moments of loneliness when my ideals did not align with popular opinion. Yet, the strength I gained from aligning with the right company far outweighed any fleeting discomfort. Surrounding myself with positive, purpose-driven individuals created a support system that reinforced my ambitions and kept me on track.

I owe a great deal of who I am today to my parents. They gave me the most precious gift a child could receive: freedom. They trusted me to make my own decisions, even from an early age. While many parents might hesitate to relinquish such control, my parents had faith in me. That trust, in turn, inspired me to earn and uphold their confidence.

Their approach gave me space to explore, make mistakes, and learn. I did not feel stifled by fear of judgment or failure. Instead, I was empowered to navigate life's complexities with curiosity and determination. That freedom shaped my resilience and adaptability—qualities that would serve me well in facing life's inevitable challenges.

Looking back, I see how profoundly my teachers influenced my life. During my primary and secondary school years, I had the privilege of learning from educators who genuinely cared about their students. These teachers did not simply see their roles as jobs; they viewed them as callings. They noticed my interests and abilities and went out of their way to nurture them. Whether it was encouraging me to ask questions, guiding me towards resources, or simply believing in my potential, their mentorship was transformative. They saw in me possibilities I had not yet imagined for myself, and their encouragement became the foundation upon which I built my ambitions.

Their lessons extended beyond the classroom, teaching me the value of discipline, perseverance, and intellectual curiosity. They instilled in me the belief that education is not just about acquiring knowledge but about cultivating wisdom and understanding tools for navigating life, not just earning a living.

Books have been a constant source of inspiration and education throughout my life. I gravitated towards works that aligned with my goals and aspirations, and they, in turn, helped shape my mindset. I read stories of resilience, guides on personal development, and insights from great thinkers.

One book changed the trajectory of my life: *How to Win Friends and Influence People* by Dale Carnegie (as mentioned earlier in this book). Its principles resonated deeply, teaching me the art of building meaningful relationships and leading with empathy. The lessons I gleaned from its pages helped me navigate both personal and professional landscapes with confidence and grace.

Through books, I found mentors I had never met, authors who opened doors to new worlds and ideas. They empowered me to think critically, act decisively, and dream boldly. Each book became a stepping-stone in growth, guiding me toward the person I aspired to be.

One of the most transformative skills I acquired was the ability to ask the right questions and seek answers from the right people. I learned that humility is the key to learning; by setting aside my ego, I could absorb wisdom from those more knowledgeable than me. This approach opened countless doors. The more curious and respectful I was in my interactions, the more willing people were to share their expertise and invest in my growth. This practice of valuing the time and wisdom of others continues to be a cornerstone of my success.

I noticed that when I demonstrated a sincere interest in learning, the "right teachers" appeared, often going beyond the usual expectations to guide me. This reciprocal relationship became a cornerstone of my learning process.

Respect for teachers and mentors was deeply ingrained in me, thanks to my cultural upbringing. I saw every mentor and teacher as a gateway to wisdom and treated them with immense regard. This respect was not limited to formal education; it extended to anyone who shared knowledge or inspired growth in me.

The value I placed on respect for others naturally translated into valuing their time. I understood that when someone offered their time and expertise, it was a gift. In return, I made every effort to show gratitude by being prepared, attentive, and committed to applying what I learned.

From an early age, I made integrity a guiding principle. I believed in honouring my commitments, delivering on my promises, and being honest in all my dealings. This was not always easy because there were times when keeping a promise required extra effort or sacrifice, but the trust and confidence I earned from others with that sacrifice made it worthwhile.

People began to see me as someone they could rely on, and this reputation opened doors to opportunities and relationships that would have otherwise been out of reach. Integrity, I found, was not just about doing what was right but about building the trust that fuels meaningful connections and lasting success.

If there is one thing that has exponentially shaped my growth, it is the ability to embrace and leverage technology. From the internet to artificial intelligence, I have been an avid student of technological advancements. Platforms like Google, Wikipedia, YouTube, and social media have been transformative tools in my journey of self-improvement and contribution to others.

I have always believed that technology itself is not the problem; it is how people choose to use it. Just as a tool can be used to build or destroy, technology can empower or harm based on the intentions behind its use. My approach has been to learn, adapt, and use technology responsibly, ensuring it aligns with my goals and values.

For example, online platforms have allowed me to learn new skills, connect with people around the world, and share my knowledge with a global audience. These tools have amplified my ability to contribute to others and grow as a person as well. I am deeply grateful for the innovators and visionaries behind these technologies; they have made it possible for people like me to expand our horizons and pursue opportunities that once seemed unattainable.

Secondly, I have always believed in the principles of fairness and justice. These values have been a compass, helping me navigate both personal and professional challenges. Treating others with fairness means recognising their humanity, respecting their rights, and ensuring that my actions contribute to, rather than detract from, a just society.

I also believe that freedom in any society comes with a responsibility. While we have the liberty to make choices, those choices should be guided by a sense of accountability–not only to ourselves but to the community around us. This balance between freedom and responsibility has shaped how I live and interact with the world.

Gratitude has been a cornerstone of my character as well. From an early age, I learned to appreciate the people, opportunities, and moments that enriched my life. Whether it was my parents' support, a teacher's guidance, or even a challenge that taught me resilience, I cultivated the habit of saying "thank you" in my heart and in my actions. Gratitude, I believe, is transformative, shifting the focus from what we lack to what we have, fostering a mindset of abundance and positivity. Practising gratitude has made me more aware of life's blessings and strengthened my relationships by allowing me to recognise and appreciate the efforts of others.

Discipline has been another defining value in my life. Whether it was waking up early to study, committing to professional growth, or maintaining a healthy lifestyle, discipline has been the bridge between my goals and achievements. Hard work is a non-negotiable component of success.

Discipline is not about rigidity but about making consistent choices that align with your values and long-term vision. It is waking up each day with a sense of purpose and doing what needs to be done, even when it is difficult or inconvenient.

Faith has always been a guiding light for me too. While I was born into a culture deeply rooted in Buddhist values, I have always embraced a broader sense of spirituality, respecting all religions and philosophies that promote peace and harmony.

Meditation and introspection became key practices that helped me connect with my inner self and navigate life's complexities. Spirituality gave me the strength to endure hardships, the clarity to make decisions, and the compassion to treat others with kindness.

I have often said that learning does not end with formal education; it is a lifelong endeavour. My belief in the power of knowledge has been a driving force behind my journey. From reading books and attending seminars to leveraging technology for self-improvement, I have always sought to expand my understanding of the world. The willingness to learn kept me adaptable in the face of change, allowing me to navigate new industries, embrace innovation, and find creative solutions to problems. Lifelong learning is not just about acquiring knowledge: it is about staying curious, open, and humble.

Life has tested me many times, but each challenge reinforced my belief in resilience. I learned that adversity is not meant to break us but to build us. Setbacks taught me patience, failure taught me perseverance, and loss taught me the value of cherishing what truly matters and reminded me of the law of impermanence. Resilience, for me, is the ability to rise after every fall, more muscular and wiser. It is about maintaining hope when things seem impossible and trusting that every storm will eventually pass.

From an early age, I realised the importance of having a vision. A clear sense of direction has always kept me motivated, even in the face of uncertainty. I set goals not just as targets but as milestones that reflect my values and aspirations. This habit of setting goals, breaking them into actionable steps, and staying committed has been a key driver of my accomplishments. Vision gives life purpose, and goals give it structure.

I believe that what has happened to us is the past, unchangeable and immutable. What truly defines us, however, is what we choose to do with those experiences. In my own journey, I have refused to adopt a victim mentality or allow myself to be confined by the words or actions of others. This mindset has given me the freedom to transform adversity into opportunity.

Life hands us all challenges, but the power to frame those challenges lies within us. By choosing to see setbacks as lessons or stepping-stones, we reclaim our agency and pave the way for growth. Adversity, when approached with the right mindset, becomes a catalyst for resilience and reinvention.

I hold a deep belief in the body's innate ability to heal when provided with the right environment and resources. Nutrition, rest, emotional well-being, and stress management are all critical components of this healing process. Our role is to respect and nurture this natural wisdom by making choices that align with our body's needs. Healing is not always immediate, but when we consistently provide the necessary "ingredients," the body's potential to recover and thrive is remarkable.

The mind and body are inseparable, intricately linked by an ongoing dialogue. Every thought we create has the power to generate physiological changes in our bodies. The more intense the thought–positive or negative–the more profound the impact on our physical state. This understanding has taught me the importance of nurturing positive thinking and guarding against harmful thought patterns. Our mindset is not just a driver of emotional well-being but a contributor to physical health as well.

One of the most liberating truths I have discovered is that our happiness is our own responsibility. No one else has the power to make us truly happy, nor should they bear that burden. By taking ownership of our happiness, we stop waiting for external conditions to align and begin cultivating joy from within. This means focusing on what we can control, our thoughts, attitudes, and actions, and letting go of the need to control others.

Life has its own seasons, much like nature. Each season, whether a time of growth, challenge, or rest, brings its own lessons and opportunities. When we align our actions with the natural rhythm of these seasons, we find balance and fulfilment.

Understanding life's seasons means embracing change and adjusting our efforts to suit the moment. It is about doing the right things at the right time and trusting that every season has its purpose.

Never put others down to make yourself feel better or superior. Instead, focus on recognising and appreciating the positive qualities in people. Speak about their strengths and highlight their good sides, as doing so will not only uplift them but also elevate your own sense of worth and character. By building others up, you naturally grow into a better and bigger person, creating a more positive and supportive environment for everyone around you.

Begin by giving to others the very thing you desire or crave for yourself. Whether it is love, respect, kindness, or support, offering it selflessly creates a powerful ripple effect. You will be amazed to see how the universe mirrors your generosity, returning it to your manifold and often in ways you never expected. Giving not only fulfils others but also enriches your own soul, making the journey truly rewarding.

These beliefs form the foundation of how I approach life. They have guided my decisions, shaped my relationships, and fuelled my growth. By choosing to take responsibility for our perspectives, emotions, and actions, we reclaim the power to live intentionally. Let us embrace these truths, not just as ideas but as tools for transformation, thereby creating a life filled with purpose, resilience, and joy.

Life experiences also show that those who used threatening, even violent, means and relied on questionable philosophical narratives to bring about change in society may achieve their purposes using legitimate, peaceful, and legal means. This is exemplified by the fact that in late 2024, the Janatha Vimukthi Peramuna (JVP), responsible for the insurrection in 1989, used the democratic process to gain political power in Sri Lanka.

In my autobiography, I have described my life of opportunity, achievements, and failure, but also of resilience, dedication, determination, and hard work. This autobiography has shown that there is a seed of greatness within each person. This seed needs to be nurtured to bloom and bring the best out of people. It is thus appropriate to finish my autobiography with a poem, written on 26 December 2024, and titled *The Seed Within*.

The Seed Within

Within each heart, a seed does lie,

A spark of greatness, reaching sky-high.

An exponential force, a boundless flame,

A potential to rise, to carve your name.

Whatever path you dare to choose,

Victory's yours if you refuse to lose.

But first, pause and ask what you seek,

What fuels your soul, what makes you unique?

Know your "why," let it burn so bright,

A compass to guide you through the night.

Honour those who walk beside your way,

For respect and kindness will light your day.

The universe flows with laws so grand.

Unseen threads guide every hand.

Embrace their wisdom, stand in awe,

For we are all part of a greater law.

See the good in all, in dark and light.

In every challenge, find insight.

Adversity whispers, "Learn and grow,'

Failure's just a stepping-stone, you know.

When storms rage fierce, and hope seems thin,

Remember the power lies within.

Hold fast, stand tall, let courage cup,

A single cry: "Don't give up! Don't give up!!"

Your seed will bloom, your greatness shine,

With every step, you define your design.

Rise and inspire, the world to see,

The extraordinary human you're meant to be.

Sarath Jayawardana

PRACTICAL INSIGHTS FOR READERS

This section of my autobiography is crafted with the sincere hope of sharing the principles, values, and beliefs that have been instrumental in shaping my life. These guiding elements have served as a foundation for my decisions, actions, and growth over the years. My hope is that they resonate with you, providing insights or inspiration to help guide you on your own unique journey. Let these words serve not just as a reflection of my experiences but also as a beacon for your own path forward.

- **Choose Your Company Wisely.** Your environment shapes your perspective. Surround yourself with people who uplift, inspire, and challenge you to be your best. It is not about excluding others but about prioritising relationships that align with your values and aspirations.

- **Build Trust with Freedom.** Whether as a parent, mentor, or leader, granting freedom with trust can unlock potential. For individuals, embracing this freedom means making choices that honour the confidence others place in you.

- **Seek Mentors Who Care.** Identify people who genuinely believe in your potential. Their guidance can help you discover talents you did not know you had and pave the way for opportunities you might not have imagined.

- **Read with Purpose.** Choose books that resonate with your goals. A single book can spark a transformation, offering tools, perspectives, and wisdom that remain with you for a lifetime.

- **Embrace Lifelong Learning.** Learning does not stop with formal education. Every interaction, challenge, and experience offer an opportunity to grow. Approach life with curiosity; you will find lessons in the most unexpected places.

- **Ask Questions with Purpose.** Identify what you want to learn and who is best equipped to teach you. Approach them with humility and genuine curiosity. People are more likely to invest in your growth when they see your eagerness to learn.

- **Respect Time, Yours and Others.** Value the time others give you by being prepared and engaged. Similarly, treat your own time as a precious resource and use it to align with your goals.

- **Keeping Your Promises and Honouring Your Commitments Builds Trust.** Integrity is a long-term investment in relationships and reputation–assets that are invaluable in life.

- **Harness Technology for Good.** Learn to use technological tools as enablers of growth. Whether it is for learning, connecting, or creating, approach technology with purpose and responsibility.

- **Balance Freedom with Responsibility.** Freedom is not a license to act without consequences. Every choice we make impacts those around us. Embrace your liberty with a commitment to fairness and justice.

- **Practice Gratitude.** Start each day by acknowledging three things you're grateful for. It could be as simple as a sunny day or as profound as the support of a loved one. Gratitude fosters positivity and strengthens relationships.

- **Cultivate Discipline.** Create daily routines that align with your values and goals. Discipline is not about perfection; it is about consistency and making small, meaningful choices every day.

- **Embrace Spirituality.** Whether through prayer, meditation, or introspection, find practices that help you connect with your inner self and the world around you. Spirituality is a source of strength and clarity.

- **Seek Opportunities to Learn, Whether Through Books, Courses, or Conversations.** Staying curious and open-minded will keep you adaptable and empowered.

- **Build Resilience.** When faced with challenges, remind yourself that setbacks are temporary and often teach valuable lessons. Trust in your ability to overcome difficulties and grow stronger.

- **Foster Empathy.** Practice active listening and try to understand others' perspectives. Empathy is not just about kindness–it is about connection and mutual respect.

- **Define Your Vision.** Spend time reflecting on what truly matters to you. Set goals that reflect your values and take deliberate steps to achieve them. A clear vision will keep you focused and motivated.

- **Reframe Challenges.** Practice seeing obstacles as opportunities for growth. Ask yourself, "What can I learn from this?"

- **Practice Agency.** Remind yourself that while you cannot control what happens, you can control how you respond.

- **Focus on the Present.** Let go of past grievances. Direct your energy towards what you can build today.

- **Assume Positive Intent,** Approach interactions with the belief that others are doing their best.

- **Empathy Practice.** Pause to consider the challenges or limitations others might be facing.

- **Let Go of Judgment.** Release the need to control how others act or think.

- **Nourish Wisely.** Prioritise a balanced diet rich in nutrients.

- **Rest and Rejuvenate.** Ensure your body receives the rest it needs to repair itself.

- **Stress Management.** Incorporate practices like meditation or mindfulness to reduce stress, which hinders healing.

- **Positive Visualisation.** Spend a few moments daily visualising positive outcomes or practice loving kindness meditation.

- **Monitor Your Inner Dialogue.** Replace negative self-talk with affirmations, encouragement, and wholesome thought.

- **Choose Your Words carefully.**

- **Set Personal Joy Goals.** Identify activities or habits that genuinely bring you happiness and prioritise them.

- **Release Expectations.** Stop relying on others to fulfil your emotional needs.

- **Cultivate Inner Peace.** Spend time in reflection or meditation to build a foundation of internal contentment.

- **Release Old Grudges.** Write down things you have been holding onto and consciously let them go.

- **Embrace Uncertainty.** Accept that not everything needs to be within your control.

- **Focus on What Matters.** Prioritise what truly adds value to your life.

- **Recognise Your Season.** Reflect on whether you are in a period of planting, harvesting, or resting.

- **Embrace Change.** Adapt your efforts to suit the season you are in.

- **Trust the Journey.** Have faith that each phase is preparing you for the next.

Remember that you have the potential to create your future and destiny. You can craft a meaningful, impactful existence with intention, humility, and determination.

Acknowledgments

Writing this book has been a deeply personal journey, and I am profoundly grateful to everyone who has supported and encouraged me along the way.

I extend my heartfelt thanks to Thilak Senaviratne for his generosity in capturing the photography for the cover and to Sifian Saeed for his expertise in typesetting and cover design.

A special acknowledgment to Venerable Ajahn Brahm for his wisdom and kindness in taking the time to read my manuscript. His words, "Your autobiography does not need improvement, no more than a gnarled and twisted tree does – it is beautiful as it is," were a profound reminder of the beauty in authenticity.

I am also deeply grateful to those who took time from their busy schedules to review this book and to everyone who has supported me in countless ways—whether by reading these pages, offering feedback, or simply believing in my journey.

With heartfelt appreciation,

Sarath Jayawardana

Perth, Australia

About the Author

Dr. Sarath Jayawardana is a multi-faceted professional with an illustrious career spanning medicine, law, education, and leadership. Holding a PhD, MD, LLB, a graduate diploma in education, a graduate diploma in legal practice, and a diploma in leadership and management, Dr. Jayawardana has dedicated his life to empowering individuals and making a meaningful impact across diverse fields. He is also a Fellow of the Australian Institute of Management (WA), attributing his commitment to excellence in leadership and organisational development.

Born and raised in Sri Lanka, Dr. Jayawardana witnessed firsthand the resilience required to navigate life's challenges, including the tumultuous 1989 Janatha Vimukthi Peramuna (JVP) upsurge—a chapter he chronicles with deep reflection in this autobiography. His personal experiences have shaped his profound commitment to justice, compassion, and personal growth.

As a new migrant to Australia, Dr. Jayawardana faced multiple challenges, including a legal battle a short time after his arrival to Australia and a health challenge a few months after stepping down from his positions as the Dean of Studies and CEO of his educational institute. This autobiography highlights his resilience, commitment, and courage in navigating these challenges and opportunities. It also underscores the lessons he learned and the values and beliefs that have shaped him into the person he is today.

Over thirty-four years in Australia, Dr. Jayawardana has trained over a thousand students from various walks of life in health and wellness areas through his educational establishments. This work has been a cornerstone of his contributions to society, emphasising his dedication to improving the lives of others through knowledge and empowerment.

When not engaged in professional endeavours, Dr. Jayawardana writes on topics close to his heart, including mind-body medicine, contemporary social, health and wellness issues, philosophy, legal insights, and leadership development. He also shares his reflections and expertise through his personal website, sarathjayawardana.com, where he continues to empower people through knowledge and inspiration.

This autobiography is a testament to his belief in the power of resilience, self-discovery, and the enduring human spirit.

www.ingramcontent.com/pod-product-compliance
Lightning Source LLC
Chambersburg PA
CBHW042319090526
44583CB00025BA/3144